Mystic Journey

MYSTIC JOURNEY

GETTING TO THE HEART OF YOUR SOUL'S STORY

ROBERT ATKINSON

COSIMOBOOKS

NEW YORK

The brief compilation of Marion Woodman's writings on soul and soul-making in the Foreword is taken from the following works: *Coming Home to Myself* (San Francisco: Conari Press, 2001), pp. 4, 209, 247; Dancing in the Flames (Boston: Shambhala, 1997), p. 37; Conscious Femininity (Toronto: Inner City Books, 1993), pp. 71, 79, 134; and *http://www.banyen.com/INFOCUS/WOODMAN.HTM*

Cover design by www.popshopstudio.com.
Interior design by www.popshopstudio.com.
ISBN: 978-1-61640-715-5

Cosimo aims to publish books that inspire, inform, and engage readers worldwide. We use innovative print-on-demand technology that enables books to be printed based on specific customer needs. This approach eliminates an artificial scarcity of publications and allows us to distribute books in the most efficient and environmentally sustainable manner. Cosimo also works with printers and paper manufacturers who practice and encourage sustainable forest management, using paper that has been certified by the FSC, SFI, and PEFC whenever possible.

Ordering Information:
Cosimo publications are available at online bookstores. They may also be purchased for educational, business, or promotional use:
Bulk orders: Special discounts are available on bulk orders for reading groups, organizations, businesses, and others.
Custom-label orders: We offer selected books with your customized cover or logo of choice.

For more information, contact us at:

Cosimo, Inc.
P.O. Box 416, Old Chelsea Station
New York, NY 10011

info@cosimobooks.com

or visit us at:
www.cosimobooks.com

TABLE OF CONTENTS

PART THREE: RECLAIMING OUR COMMON SPIRITUAL HERITAGE

You know the value of every article of
merchandise,
but if you don't know the value of your own soul,
it's all foolishness.
You've come to know the fortunate and the
inauspicious stars,
but you don't know whether you yourself
are fortunate or unlucky.
This, this is the essence of all sciences—
that you should know who you will be
when the Day of Reckoning arrives.

—Rumi[1]

FOREWORD

SOUL-MAKING IS WHEN TIME MEETS THE TIMELESS

by Marion Woodman

Psychological work is soul work. Psychology is the science of the psyche, of the soul. Having looked at so many dreams for so many years, I cannot deny that a process guides the soul. By soul, I mean the eternal part of us that lives in this body for a few years, the timeless part of ourselves that wants to create timeless objects like art, painting, and architecture.

The creative process for me is extremely important. Whenever the ego surrenders to the archetypal images of the unconscious, time meets the timeless. Insofar as those moments are conscious, they are psychological—they belong to the soul. They are in time, illuminating, not rejecting, the timeless.

I see soul as the embodied part. I see spirit as the energy, the disembodied energy that can come into union with the soul in the body. For example, a great dancer like Nureyev can prepare his instrument. His muscles can be in perfect shape through his attention and his concentration. So, his consciousness, his light in his body—which for me would be soul—can be a perfect instrument. But, he's a great dancer when spirit is in union with that instrument. The leap is in the union of soul and spirit.

In the first half of life, we live mainly in terms of *doing*. We find out who we are through going to school, pursuing a career, marrying, having children, and raising them. In the second half of life, we are pushed toward a deeper consciousness of who we are, an identity in terms of *being*, an identity based not on the ego but on the soul.

Soul-making is allowing the eternal essence to live and experience the outer world through all the senses—seeing, smelling, hearing, tasting, touching—so that the soul grows during its time on Earth. Soul-making is constantly confronting the paradox that an eternal being is dwelling in a temporal body. That's why it suffers, and learns by heart. Soul hears with eternal ears, sees with eternal eyes, smells with eternal nose. Yet, having no tongue, other than the transitory language of the body, it learns to speak in metaphor.

When it comes to pain, we don't want it; so we avoid it in any possible way we can. I see this culture in terms of addictions. An addict can be blind to the death wish that is killing him, or he can open his eyes and choose life. As people on this planet we can do the same thing—we can choose to live in the Garden or we can destroy it. We can either stupidly proclaim that we are all-powerful; there is no miracle out there; there is no life force that we have to bow to. Or we can humbly acknowledge that there is an incredible mystery creating all those different life forms.

When they finally decided to build a monument in Washington [to the Vietnam War], a woman designed a black wall that goes deep into Mother Earth, and on it is inscribed every name of every casualty. Finally America has its Wailing Wall. People come to the wall and feel the names of their loved ones with their fingers, their bodies, and they weep. That's what war is about—tears. And that's what real life is about—suffering, loss, conflict, joy. The dark and the light. What Keats called the "vale of soul-making."

One thing has been distilled in my consciousness. By whatever name we call the two magnets that create this balance of energies in our bodies and in our planet—masculine/feminine, Shiva/Shakti, Yang/Yin, Spirit/Soul, Transcendence/Immanence, Doing/Being, we are now responsible for making space for the healing of body, soul, and spirit. We are being directed in the evolutionary process by divine guides through our dreams, our symptoms, our planet. New values are emerging—feminine values and masculine values that are free of patriarchal abuse. A totally new harmonic lies ahead in the new millennium.

If we believe in a divine order, then everything, everything on the Earth, is part of that divine order. We're all little sparks of One Soul. We are "ensouled" on this planet. And once that comes through to consciousness, we understand what love is. The atoms are held together by love; love is the glue that holds it all together. Maybe that's what the new millennium will be about, realizing that we are all ensouled in One Soul.

I do believe in Divine Providence. I don't think that the globe could have evolved this far only to be annihilated. My sense is that this chaos that we're going through could go on for a long time yet—that maybe we're only at the beginning of the real chaos. But when we finally come to our knees, something else will happen. We might realize that we are one people inhabiting one country—that we are all part of One Soul. That we do belong. That we are all part of one cosmos.

True creativity, true soul-making, comes from that deep communication with what Jung would call the archetypal world. That's where the real nourishment is. When we connect with our souls, we connect with the soul of every human being. We resonate with all living things.

When things are investigated, knowledge is extended;
When knowledge is extended, the will becomes sincere;
When the will is sincere, the mind is rectified;
When the mind is rectified, the personal life is cultivated;
When the personal life is cultivated, the family will be regulated;
When the family is regulated, the state will be in order;
And when the state is in order, there will be peace throughout the world.
—Confucius[2]

A CONTEXT FOR THE MYSTIC JOURNEY AND PRACTICAL SOUL-MAKING

After nine months [in the womb], the angel returns one final time
to tell the soul, "The time has come for you to go forth into the world."
But the soul objects strenuously, saying, "No, I like it here. Why should I go?"
The angel replies, "As you were formed against your will,
so shall you be born against your will and you will die against your will."
The soul continues to resist, but is brought forth into the world anyway,
kicking and screaming. Immediately the child forgets all it has learned.
—From the Jewish legend, "The Angel and the Unborn Soul"[3]

When all the souls had chosen their lives . . . without turning round they passed beneath the throne of Necessity . . . They marched on in a scorching heat to the plain of Forgetfulness . . . then towards evening they encamped by the river of Unmindfulness. Of this they were all obliged to drink a certain quantity . . . and each one as he drank forgot all things. Now after they had gone to rest, about the middle of the night there was a thunderstorm and earthquake, and then in an instant they were driven upwards in all manner of ways to their birth, like stars shooting.
—Plato[4]

How then are Souls to be made? How then are these sparks which are God to have identity given them—so as ever to possess a bliss peculiar to each one's individual existence? How, but by the medium of a world like this?

—John Keats[5]

How many of us . . . have really been . . . prepared for the second half of life, for old age, death and eternity?

—C. G. Jung[6]

INTRODUCTION

WHO WE ARE IS WHERE WE CAME FROM

Do you not see how necessary a World of Pains and troubles
is to school an Intelligence and make it a soul?
—John Keats[7]

The whole world and all of life
are nothing but the raw materials for soul-making.
—Thomas Moore[8]

As human beings, we are all tied together by the same spiritual DNA. We realize that our lives have always been sacred when we are drawn into the timelessness of the human experience. We do this by connecting with the eternal, or what is most essentially human, when we see that our own experience or situation in life is not unique, but is common to others and is timeless.

Beyond all the here-and-now stuff of our lives, we all come from a common origin, someplace deeper and longer-lasting than this surface level existence. Beyond the daily, mundane events of our lives, everyone also has an eternal soul.

Marion Woodman says, "When we connect with our souls, we connect with the soul of every human being. We resonate with all living things." This is usually a newly perceived connection that only comes through life lived deeply. She also says, "Real life is about suffering, loss, conflict, joy. The dark and the light. What Keats called the 'vale of soul-making.'"[9]

As a young English teacher, Marion Woodman knew Keats before she knew C. G. Jung and James Hillman. She also knew that Keats was talking about "learning life by heart." If we do come from an eternal place, where spirit prevails, being thrust into this material realm would cause quite a bit of turmoil and conflict, just what Keats says the soul, a spark of God, needs to form its new identity.

Rather than viewing life on Earth as a "vale of tears," as in the traditional Christian perspective, in which the world provided an experience of darkness and suffering that we could escape only through divine redemption, Keats preferred to "call the world if you Please 'The vale of Soul-making.'" He believed there is a greater purpose to our time in this world, and that our true and lasting identity was formed through the lessons learned from life's most challenging experiences:[10]

> There may be intelligences or sparks of the divinity in millions—but they are not Souls till they acquire identities, till each one is personally itself... How then are Souls to be made? How then are these sparks [which are God]... to have identity given them—so as ever to possess a bliss peculiar to each one's individual existence? How, but by the medium of a world like this? . . . Do you not see how necessary a World of Pains and troubles is to school an Intelligence and make it a soul? A Place where the heart must feel and suffer in a thousand diverse ways! . . . As various as the Lives of Men are—so various become their Souls, and thus does God make individual beings, Souls, Identical Souls of the sparks of his own essence.

Soul-making happens when the light merges with the dark, when joy and sorrow intermingle, when the eternal breaks through from the temporal realm, and when polarities are consciously acknowledged and confronted in our everyday lives.

When these opposites are experienced, and their lessons are learned, here in the classroom of the world, the soul remembers what it came here for and evolves as it is designed to. As the woodcarver who sees the carving he wants to fashion even before he starts to carve the wood, soul -making is a process revealing what is already there.

All of the temporal chaos, confusion, conflict, and suffering that results from the interaction of opposites in this world is the only thing that truly serves as a catalyst for personal change, growth, and transformation. The stuff that only this material world can provide us, the deep and jarring contrast between the temporal and the eternal, is the necessary stuff of soul-making.

For C. G. Jung, the psyche was the soul, and the soul is what links us to the archetypal world. Soul-making is all about communicating deeply with the inner realm, or being fully awake and aware as the numinous bursts forth from the unconscious, flooding our consciousness with eternal images. He wrote: "My life is a story of the self-realization of the unconscious. Everything in the unconscious seeks outward manifestation, and the personality too desires to evolve out of its unconscious conditions and to experience itself as a whole . . . I can understand myself only in the light of inner happenings. It is these that make up the singularity of my life."[11] What he is getting at here is that at our essence, we are like all other human beings. Soul-making is about experiencing the universals of life.

James Hillman would see soul-making as what happens when we evoke the emotions and experiences—of crisis and opportunity, of love and dying—that give life a deeper meaning. This could happen at any reflective moment that turns the unique into the universal, the temporal into the eternal. This requires seeing the world, with all of its opposites and dualities, as Keats did, as providing the necessary stuff of soul-making.

A deeply lived life allows us to wrestle with our demons, dance with our angels, make plans with our inner guide, and ultimately, connect with our soul. This provides us with an opportunity to exercise our imagination and to use our creative energies to transform our lives by forming mental images of what may not actually be present, but what we would like to be. "Image" and "imagination" are both from the same root, *imago*, which signifies a likeness or copy of what we envision.

We may even be born with the image of the person we become, as James Hillman contends in his intriguing "acorn theory." He says that every single person is born with a defining image, an innate uniqueness—already present *before* we are born—which asks only to be lived out with the life we are given. This innate image is our essence, yet only with the unfolding of a lifetime does this inner quality, or character defining who we are, become evident. As the mighty oak's destiny is written in the tiny acorn, so our calling, or destiny, can only be understood as we look backward, reflectively, over a life lived deliberately.[12]

We are formed from archetypal images and grow gradually into our own image of the archetype, as we age and mature through life's experiences. Another way of saying this, as many spiritual traditions do, is that we are formed in the image of God and we have the innate capacity to reflect that image in the life we live. But character and image are inseparable. Both are the essence of who we are. We get to the essence of who we are by expressing how we have originated from divinity, or how love, order, beauty, and justice, or any of the other divine qualities of the holy have been demonstrated in our own lives.[13]

We are given, as a gift, a "soul-companion," a *daimon,* which is with us each step of our journey, guiding us through the *paradeigma,* or pattern, of the life we live, toward our destiny. This acorn-like inborn essence of who we will become is given different names in different cultures and traditions, from "soul" to "genius" to "calling" to "fate" to "character." Though none really tells us exactly what it is, each confirms *that* it is, that we all have a purpose to fulfill with the life we have to live. Making sense of image has always been a function of myth, or of sacred stories.

Jung says "image *is* psyche," and he said that at a time when "psyche" still meant "soul."[14] We cannot think without relying upon inherited mental images. In the Aristotelian tradition of imagination as a fundamental quality of the mind, Jung is pointing out that memory (*memoria*) is actually a storage place that we have the ability to access and return from, bringing back eternal images to the mind.

Memory, therefore, *is* soul. Remembering, which requires imagination, is a function of the soul. The entry to this storage place is often through the doors of life review, or by telling the story of our life. We can also find images there that may be beyond our own capacity to imagine, but that nevertheless come to us from some universal wellspring, enabling us to become more than we were, or could have imagined.

Rather than indicating anything like predestination, the inborn image serves as a spark of consciousness that will benefit our own growth. It has our best interests as its purpose. Other names for this mysterious force overseeing our lives would be "grace," or "providence," what we might think of as being invisibly watched over. Going further in this direction, we could also add "guardian spirit" and hundreds of other terms, until we finally got to God as possibly the source for all of this aid and assistance.

This theory provides a blueprint for human development, or a psychology of childhood, youth, and adulthood. It affirms an inherent uniqueness, even a direction or pattern, waiting to unfold for each person at each stage of life. Each of us has an innate gift to utilize at a time meant to lead us directly to our essence, to our soul.

Could it be that it is not the *I* that looks back to review our life, but the *soul?* That is who we really are. Memory, that soulful part of us, wants all of who we are to remember; it seems to push itself on us, bringing back to consciousness vital images, scenes, figures, and feelings that help us re-member ourselves and in the process find deeper meaning and solidify soul qualities we may have long cultivated.

Could it be the *intention* of the soul to bring back, or even cause to appear for the first time, those eternal images, coupled with those soul qualities and virtues, needed to ensure our further progress in our continuing journey? We cannot escape remembering. Reviewing our life helps us form, or re-form, our deep character when we need it most, as a final conscious preparation for the soul's ultimate destination.

As Hillman clearly puts it, "Life review yields long-term gains that enrich character by bringing understanding to events. The patterns in your life become more discernible among the wreckage and the romance, more like a well-plotted novel that reveals characters through their actions and reactions . . . Without stories there is no pattern, no understanding . . . merely habits, events passing before the eyes of an aimless observer." He sees life review as "character making its claim" or as our sign that the soul "doesn't want to leave this world innocent of the life it has been living."[15]

As each of the nine Muses in the ancient myth artfully formed her values by musing upon her mother, the goddess Memory, we too can muse over our memories, let them take the shape they want, and notice how they form our values, virtues, and character. Life review is really about musing the values our life is built upon into meaningful patterns, themes, and subthemes.

The necessary, essential context for soul-making is life's difficulties and struggles, as these are what contribute most to meaning making and pattern shaping. With time, the unpleasant becomes more pleasant, old hurts don't hurt as much, and what once felt cold becomes warmer. The soul naturally wants to lighten up in preparation for an easier lift-off. Could this vital work, Hillman asks, be the soul's "premonition of what religious traditions call heaven"? This is where the rest of the book is headed.

Soul-making is about preparing for our reunion with our Creator; it is a lifelong process of acquiring the attributes needed for our eternal journey—a process that also leads to both individual and collective transformation.

The book expands upon the idea that our lives—our spiritual existence from before birth to after death—may reflect a process of *knowing*, *forgetting*, and *remembering*. According to a number of sacred traditions, we may have had a kind of an innate *knowing* about our life to come before we came into this world. But our physical birth seems to have initiated a *forgetting* of what we could have once known, so we spend the rest of our lives *remembering* what we forgot in order to come into the *knowing* we started out with. Remembering is a way of getting back in touch with our soul, the source of that knowing; it actually represents the search within our selves for the ancient mysteries of creation, what Jung might include as part of the collective unconscious.

Those moments of wonder we've all had when something happens at just the right time to make it seem like we already knew what we just learned—sort of like *déjà vu*—are part of a cognitive process of being tuned into our soul. The soul is the storehouse of eternal memories. The more we can identify with our eternal self, rather than with our temporal self, the more we will be able to learn from our soul about its stored memories. Living from our soul rather than from our physical self means not always needing to be in control: it is listening more, trying to hear and understand what our intuitions and emotions have to tell us, keeping our eyes on the whole more than on the parts, being as concerned for others as we are for ourselves, connecting with nature and remaining as much in sync with its natural rhythms and cycles as we possibly can, and remembering that our soul is our only lasting identity, the one that is given to us before birth and that we will take with us on the rest of our eternal journey. What the soul wants from us is to be remembered as that changeless, eternal part of us.[16]

So, the important question is not, what do *I* want, but rather, what *is wanted* beyond my current consciousness? What does my soul *want*? What are my deepest longings? What is the spirit of my life? What is most sacred to me? Giving narrative voice to these questions is essential for practical soul-making and achieving wholeness.

The first part of the book looks at remembrance as a spiritual practice, how we are hardwired for transcendence, how we can use our conscious powers to remember our essential spiritual nature, and why it benefits us to see our life as the eternal journey of the soul. The second part of the book examines the timeless pattern of transformation, why there is the necessity for opposition in our lives and what this contributes to transformation, and why this universal pattern can become what is personally sacred to us. Part III explores the timeless archetypes in the world's sacred traditions as the primary elements of our common spiritual heritage, explains how we are all the inheritors of this rich heritage, and describes how soul-making can help us merge our life with the spirit of our time.

The approach used here, of remembering, re-visioning, and reclaiming the nature of our soul, is practical because it prepares the eternal part of us for the next phase of its journey beyond this earthly existence. Seeing our life from this eternal perspective is practical, because it teaches us about our spiritual self, about our personal quest for wholeness and authenticity, and helps us, as Rumi indicated, to know the value of our own soul, which is very important.

The world's sacred scriptures contain much about remembering who we are, where we came from, and where we are going. This book is unique in offering both a temporal and an eternal perspective. With a life-is-an-eternal-journey perspective, our lives in the here and now take on an entirely different purpose and meaning. Remembering is a spiritual endeavor reminding us of who we are in eternity.

As is clear in the Confucian tradition, there is also a practical and direct link between the individual and the rest of the world. What the individual does to cultivate, deepen, and transform his or her own life will inevitably affect others and will spread outward, like a ripple in a pond, creating ever-widening circles of empathy from the person to the family, the community, the nation, and finally to all of humanity. Confucius understood that the highest social ethic, or the Grand Unity, is fully dependent upon the learning and the morals of each individual, as well as upon the harmony among all levels of society and among all living creatures. The never-ending work of transforming the world has its roots in personal transformation, or soul-making.

PART I

REMEMBERING WHO WE ARE

Rejoice in the Lord, ye righteous; and give thanks at the remembrance of his holiness.
—Psalms 97:1

Then he took a loaf of bread, and when he had given thanks, he broke it and gave it to them, saying, "This is my body which is given for you. Do this in remembrance of me."
—Luke 22:19

Surely in remembrance of God are all hearts comforted.
—Qur'an 33:41

CHAPTER ONE

REMEMBRANCE IS A SPIRITUAL PRACTICE

As from a blazing fire sparks, being like unto fire, fly forth a thousandfold, thus are various beings brought forth from the Imperishable, my friend, and return thither also.

—Mundaka Upanishad 2, 1:1[17]

Our birth is but a sleep and a forgetting:
The Soul that rises with us, our life's Star,
Hath had elsewhere its setting,
And cometh from afar:
Not in entire forgetfulness,
And not in utter nakedness,
But trailing clouds of glory do we come
From God, who is our home:
Heaven lies about us in our infancy!
. . . Hence in a season of calm weather
Though inland far we be,
Our Souls have sight of that immortal sea
Which brought us hither,
can in a moment travel thither . . .

—William Wordsworth[18]

There is a great power in remembrance. Through remembrance we are brought to a spiritual life. Remembrance is a meditation that awakens us to an everlasting reality. The conscious effort to maintain this focus expands our view of the world and our role in it; we learn thus to better understand the conflicts that arise in our lives, to distinguish between the endless pairs of opposites that appear, to make wiser choices, and to carry out deeds that become a service to others. This, in essence, is the basis for spiritual transformation, and remembrance takes us there.

The world's sacred traditions acknowledge the importance of seeking answers to the mysteries of life. At the heart of this quest for spiritual understanding are two essential questions: "Where have we come from?" and "Where are we going?" The mystery of our origin and our destiny is intricately tied to the nature of the soul. The world's sacred traditions agree that the soul is eternal, that it exists prior to birth, and that it continues after death.

The world's religions further agree that the soul comes from and returns to God. The foundation of the Jewish tradition regarding the soul and mystic knowing is seen in Ecclesiastes (12:7), "The dust returns to the ground it came from, and the spirit returns to God who gave it." The long-standing mystical tradition of the kabbalah includes practices such as prayer, some forms of which are designed to evoke the image of God breathing the breath of life (the Holy Spirit) into man, which reflects the state of union we are born with.[19]

The Christian framework for this mystic knowing is found in 2 Corinthians (4:1, 18), where Paul speaks of the duality we experience in this world, but acknowledges the ultimate union that exists: "Now we know that if the earthly tent we live in is destroyed, we have a building from God, an eternal house in heaven, not built by human hands . . . So we fix our eyes not on what is seen but what is unseen. For what is seen is temporary, but what is unseen is eternal."

The 20th century English monk Bede Griffiths recalled the timeless mystic vision of Reality when he wrote, "There is a window in my consciousness where I can look out on eternity . . . then I discover my true Self, then I begin to see the world as it really is . . . Here all is one, united in a simple vision of being."[20]

Mystic knowing in Islam has its source in the Qur'an. Similar to the

Jewish and Christian traditions, the Qur'an speaks of our being created by God, being given a home in heaven, and emphasizes our reunion with God. The phrase, "Unto Him shall ye return," is oft repeated in the Qur'an (10:4; 19:11; 29:57–58; 31:14). The Night Journey of the Prophet to Jerusalem, and his ascent from there through the seven heavens to God, is symbolic of this return (Qur'an, 17:1). It has long been the purpose of the Sufis, in representing the mystical core of Islam, to experience and explain this journey back to God. The central Sufi doctrine of *tawhid* refers to union with God, as well as the oneness of God, and has to do with shedding attachments to the world.[21]

At the heart of the Baha'i scriptures is the belief that our purpose in this life is to prepare for the life beyond, that the soul is on a journey from and back to God: "All things proceed from God and unto Him they return." Like all other divinely revealed religions, the Baha'i Faith is fundamentally mystic in character, with the goal of developing both the individual and society, through the acquisition of virtues and ethical values.[22]

When we look at Genesis (2:7), "The Lord God formed man of the dust of the ground, and breathed into his nostrils the breath of life; and man became a living soul," the dual nature of man, physical and spiritual, is clearly evident. Created by God of both spirit and Earth, these two forms merge and interact in the human being, causing a lifelong tension between the material and the spiritual. Our dual nature can therefore be seen as the source of many of life's struggles and difficulties throughout our earthly existence. We are continually pulled by both the physical and the spiritual worlds.

How we deal with those tests and trials brought about by the physical world the soul is thrust into; how we come to this mystic knowledge of our true nature, origin, and destiny; and how we best prepare ourselves for our return to where we came from are the keys to our progress and development here. The world's sacred traditions give us the best guideposts to follow in helping us to recognize our origin as well as our destiny.

There is a story shared by many sacred traditions that addresses, most likely metaphorically, how we learn, as unborn souls, what our nature and destiny are. But, as the story goes, we are born forgetting where we came from and why we are here. Our physical nature, and its needs and wants, take over at birth, and we seem to suspend our spiritual reality. So, we spend the rest of our lives trying to remember where we have come from and what we have already forgot, as Wordsworth hints in his poem.

One example of this story is the Jewish mystical legend, "The Angel and the Unborn Soul:"[23]

> When the soul of Adam was created, the souls of all the generations were created and stored in the seventh heaven. God sends an angel to invite each soul from there to carry it to the womb of its mother. One time, when a soul is invited to come along to its mother, the soul protests, saying, "Don't take me from this place. I am well pleased here." But the angel assures it that, "The world to which you are going is better than this one, and besides, it is for this purpose that God created you." So the soul is dragged away and forcibly placed in the womb of the mother.
>
> The next day, the angel returns and takes the soul on a journey to paradise, saying that these are the righteous who were "formed like you in the wombs of their mothers," and, having followed God's commandments in the world, "when they departed that world they became partakers in the happiness that you now see," and the soul is assured that it, too, will be found worthy of abiding there if God's commandments are observed.
>
> Then the next day the angel returns to show the soul what hell is like, and on the following day returns again to show the soul what her life on earth will be like. After nine months, the angel returns one final time to tell the soul, "The time has come for you to go forth into the world." But the soul objects strenuously, saying, "No, I like it here. Why should I go?" The angel replies, "As you were formed against your will, so shall you be born against your will and you will die against your will." The soul continues to resist, but is brought forth into the world anyway, kicking and screaming. Immediately the child forgets all it has learned.

This legend addresses the descent of the soul, or its process of knowing and forgetting. Islam has a similar story about the common origin of all souls and their individual descent to Earth, in which they pass through all the basic material elements and finally become embedded in the physical body, where they remain hidden. (This also reflects the Sufi tradition of seven souls.)

"However," as the Islamic version of the story goes, "God sent with the soul the Divine Attributes so that each individual is a link between heaven and Earth. Unfortunately, once embedded in materiality, we became blind to that secret within us." But this story offers a way we can remember what we forgot. It says God also gave us the tools of "mind" and "will" to return to this original level of awareness.[24]

This legend common to many traditions may not be meant to be taken literally but rather figuratively for what is symbolically possible in this life. And we may even know of some exceptions to this process in gifted children, who may seem to be born with some remembrance of their life as a soul before birth.

But with each question answered, there are still other questions to ask. How do we remember what is buried within us? How do we use the tools within us? How do we regain access to the forgotten knowledge of our divine origin and begin our ascent back to where we came from?

Our journey of descent from the eternal worlds, characterized by knowing and forgetting, continues in this world after birth as a journey of ascent, characterized by gradually gaining consciousness and then potentially remembering what was once known in the sacred realm.

The legend of "The Angel and the Unborn Soul" takes us right to the essence of our spiritual reality. The soul is our eternal identity, the only part of us we take with us through this life and into the next. Remembrance is the essence of spirituality. Remembering where we came from, who—and what—we really are, and where we are going, could even be seen as the purpose of life.

We might say, then, that we are hard-wired for transcendence, for going beyond what is seen. Transcendence could be so important to our individual and collective spiritual growth and well-being that we might not even survive without it in our lives and our communities. One cell transcends into many; many cells transcend into one body. Individuals transcend into societies, and societies transcend into world civilizations.

As souls born into physical bodies, we may be meant to go beyond what is not only most familiar to us, but to seek that which we truly are at our innermost essence. And this process has been a very long time in the works, matter transcending into mind, and the powers of the mind transcending to a consciousness of spirit. Imagine how yet-to-come levels of consciousness could add to our capacity for transcendence.

Consciousness is a unique characteristic of the self. Einstein showed us how the apparent restrictions of time and space are only illusions of this finite earthly existence. Being hard-wired for transcendence means having the innate capacity to grasp concepts beyond our experience and to utilize our consciousness to visualize infinity or eternity, enabling us to realize the potential we were born with.

Self-transcendence is consciousness fulfilling itself. A baby is not born with full-blown consciousness. Its consciousness naturally and inevitably undergoes a widening of perspective with accompanying experiences. As we progress through the life cycle, we gain meaning and maturity with each new experience. Unfolding from within is a built-in process of transcending our own consciousness until eventually, we become conscious of the One who created consciousness.

Transcendence, then, is a process that brings individual consciousness into a closer, more connected relationship with the all-pervasive superconsciousness, or universal mind that is called God. Through this process we take on new and expanding identities, but we do not lose previous ones. We retain our personal consciousness while merging our thoughts with a universal mind. This process becomes the adventure of a lifetime, of learning how to enter the realm of the infinite.[25]

Such transcendence may also be the purpose of our lives on Earth. Self-transcendence, an educational device beyond any other, is designed to take us where we are meant to go, to the farthest reaches of what we are capable of becoming. It begins when we are still a seed soul, a fertilized egg in the womb, awaiting admission to the soul school of Earth, and does not end until we are reunited with the source of our being in the realm of the spirit. Our earthly life takes us along a path of growing awareness in an illusory space-time continuum, which becomes but an interval, a momentary note, in a song of eternal mystery, each breath of which moves us closer to an incomprehensible reunion.

REMEMBERING WHAT WE ALREADY KNOW

Transcendence and remembrance are two halves of a cyclical process. Remembrance, the conscious effort of reflecting on and listening to our thoughts in prayer and meditation, helps us to achieve transcendence. Transcendence helps us remember more of what we may have once known, as unborn souls having come from an eternal realm. As a regular practice, remembrance can help us become and remain conscious of who we are as spiritual beings, how we see ourselves in the world, and how everyday events and circumstances affect and influence us.

Oral storytelling was an essential method of education in the ways of sacred knowledge for the people in indigenous and native cultures.[26] Teaching stories often contained codes, symbols, metaphors, and allegories telling about the ordinary as well as the extraordinary, or the metaphysical and the cosmological. A conscious, reverential approach to learning and remembering was adopted. To be aware of what is going on around us and what life holds in store for us is at the heart of the spiritual practice of remembrance, as this verse from the Ute tradition illustrates: [27]

Earth, teach me stillness
  as the grasses are stilled with light.
Earth teach me suffering
  as old stones suffer with memory . . .
Earth teach me resignation
  as the leaves which die in the fall.
Earth teach me to remember kindness
  as dry fields weep with rain.

Through our various spiritual traditions, we have a variety of practices designed to keep us focused on this awareness of the pervasive sacred: the Eightfold Path, the Ten Commandments, the Sermon on the Mount, the Five Pillars, and many other rituals and ceremonies that involve regular ways to draw our attention to the sacred.

At the heart of most spiritual practice, what is left when we move beyond form, constricting language, and what may be for some the stiffness of the prescriptions, is simply remembering.[28] Remember who you are. Remember what you love. Remember what is sacred. Remember what is true. Remember that you will die, that this day is a gift. Remember how you wish to live, that you will return to where you came from.

When the prophets, such as Jesus, say "Remember me," they are really saying "Remember God, who is in us as we are in Him." This is designed to keep our focus on the sacred, on the spiritual aspect of life. This is where we will find our greatest comfort, the healing of our ills, the holiness of life, and the love that we will most cherish. One of the greatest gifts we can give ourselves is finding the practice, simple or otherwise, that will help us remember who we are, what we do know, and what we do not yet remember that we know. It can be meditation, prayer, writing, singing, walking, or even the mundane routines of life. Having such a means to keep our focus, a simple act that helps center us into a remembrance of what we already know is sacred and beautiful is essential to our spiritual growth. Simple acts of remembrance greatly enrich our spiritual life.

Remembrance can be simple and momentary, or it can be an entire review of one's life. This practice helps us not only remember the important things that add meaning to our lives, but to let go of the unimportant things, too. This helps us get to our essence. Remembrance includes the recognition of what we would not want to live without, what gives us the simplest joys in life. Remembrance is also honoring both our joys and sorrows, because surely the sorrows provide some of the greatest meaning in our lives, too. Remembrance helps us find and give a constructive meaning to what we thought were the sorrows of our lives.

But this is not an easy process. Living in the material world is like having dust gather upon the soul. As Abdu'l-Baha explains, this dust is "attachment to the world, avarice, envy, love of luxury and comfort, haughtiness and self-desire." These are some of the things that cover the light within us, and prevent "the rays of the Sun of Reality" from transforming us further into a reflection of its "intense brilliancy and radiance." What will wipe the dust away, purify us, and make us radiant again, he adds, is "sincerity, justice, humility, severance, and love" toward others. And since the soul can also be seen as "the repository of the ancient, Divine mysteries of God," remembering, through the lifelong process of soul-making, may well be the most powerful tool for achieving self-knowledge, as this knowledge is within us and accessible and essential to who we have always been and always will be.[29]

Remembrance removes the dust and allows the light within us to shine. As we mature spiritually, our remembrance grows deeper and deeper and moves us along the continuum away from material attachments and toward a state of constant remembrance of the Divine.

There is no better way of understanding the mysteries of life, the process of transformation, the will of God, or how our own lives reflect a divine plan, than by remembering the lives of the prophets, not only for the spiritual message they bring, but for the trials and tribulations they have endured in their own lives. The term "remembrance of God" in its ultimate meaning refers to "the Manifestation of God, who is the consummate symbol, representation, and reflection of the divine hidden Reality within the realm of creation," according to Nader Saiedi.[30] In knowing and remembering the prophet, we come closest to knowing God.

Baha'u'llah, the founder of the Baha'i Faith, as the latest in a long line of the prophets of God, asks us to remember him because this is what will truly be "the healer of (our) ills." Baha'u'llah wants us to remember him not only as a prophet of God, through whom we can know and love God and retain our own light, but also for an understanding of and familiarity with the universal, archetypal experiences that we will share with him: "Lament not in your hours of trial, neither rejoice therein; seek ye the Middle Way which is the remembrance of Me in your afflictions and reflection over that which may befall you in the future." And similarly, "If tribulation touch thee for My sake, call thou to mind My ills and troubles, and remember My banishment and imprisonment."[31]

By remembering his days, all the trials and hardships they consisted of, during our times of difficulties, we bring greater meaning to our own lives, and recognize more clearly the purpose in everything that befalls us. Within the prophets' own real-life experiences are a reflection of ours. As they overcame the severest of suffering, so can we; as their tests ultimately contributed to their life purpose, so do ours.

Baha'u'llah experienced the same challenges, tribulations, and persecutions in his life as did prior prophets.[32] And, as was often the case, it was under the worst of circumstances that he showed the greatest courage and achieved his greatest honor. Though he did not personally set out to reveal the word of God, it was in submitting to the will of God, which included severe tests and difficulties, that he was moved to speak the word of God, revealed unbidden to him.

Baha'u'llah's life experience not only consists of perpetual change and multiple transformations occurring out of times hardship and persecution, it also expresses very vividly how the forces of opposition in conflict with each other paradoxically and dialectically merge to transcend the difficulty at hand. This is a pattern illustrated clearly in the lives of all prophets, as well as in the lives of the world's mythic gods and goddesses and heroes and heroines. This theme of the pattern and process of transformation is taken up in Chapter 3 as the most important archetypal experience we can have in our lives. This is also why Baha'u'llah asks us to remember his days, so that we will become even more familiar with the essential role of struggle and transformation in our lives.

REMEMBRANCE IS LIVING IN GRATITUDE

Remembrance is a meditation that creates gratitude, gratefulness, and strength of faith; this is essential preparation for spiritual transformation. Our greatest lessons of spiritual transformation come directly from the real lives of the prophets, from Krishna, Moses, Zoroaster, Buddha, Christ, Muhammad, and from Baha'u'llah. We nurture our own spiritual lives by remembering the lives of the prophets, the wondrous attributes and qualities they expressed, and the tremendous struggles and hardships they endured. This helps us remember own spiritual essence and potential, and that we will experience similar motifs of joy and sorrow, crisis and victory, and light and shadow in our lives, too.

The mystic traditions all exist to help us remember what we forgot about our true origin and destiny. The journey of descent is one of forgetting; that of ascent, one of remembering. The mystic way and *The Seven Valleys* (to be taken up in the next chapter), describe, step by step, this eternal journey of the soul.

The soul's greatest challenge, not that surprisingly, is with the physical body it is connected to on its journey through this world. The constant pull between the physical and spiritual realms creates a series of trials and tribulations for both. Our daily discipline *in the world* is our training ground. The prophets make it clear that our call is to worldly action. Not escape *from* the world, but work *in* the world, is the real goal. There is a distinct service orientation to spiritual growth and the ascent of the soul.

The ancient legends, shedding light on the unborn soul, tell us that we already know where we came from and where we are going. The part of us that always remembers, that always lives in close proximity to God, is called the "secret soul" in the Sufi tradition.[33] Our remembrance of where we came from and where we are going will fundamentally change us and will transform all our relationships into relationships of authenticity, respect, and compassion.

The great mystic poets, too, knew that remembrance links us to the spirit we all possess, which links us to each other, as well. Rumi puts it this way:[34]

What I tell about "me" I tell about you
The walls between us long ago burned down
This voice seizing me is your voice
Burning to speak to us of us.

And Walt Whitman says:[35]

I celebrate myself;
And what I assume you shall assume;
For every atom belonging to me, as good belongs to you.

The practice of the remembrance of God is a practice common to all sacred traditions. The pursuit of remembering one's true origin, identity, and destiny should not lead to "idleness and seclusion," but to yielding fruit, to serving God and humanity, through deeds. Baha'u'llah states, "True remembrance is to make mention of the Lord, the All-Praised, and forget aught else beside Him."[36] This implies active, rather than passive, remembrance; it involves a two-part process of remembering what was forgotten and then making mention of God to others through our own deeds and actions that benefit and serve others.

If we consciously remembered where we came from before this life and where we are going after this life, we could dramatically alter each moment of our existence during this lifetime. Seeing our life within an eternal framework would give us a very different perspective, possibly even seeing it as "a fleeting moment" as mystics do.[37]

There is a direct link between the Jewish legend of the unborn soul, the practice of the remembrance of God, and the Hasidic story of Rabbi Zusya, who gets to the end of his life with a great question unanswered. If we did automatically remember what we experienced as an unborn soul, this story would not even have come into existence. But since we do spend a good portion of our lives remembering who we are, we do have this companion story and its warning, which in a way picks up where the legend of the angel and the unborn soul left off. That legend is about the soul's descent to this earthly plane of existence; the story of Rabbi Zusya is about the soul's ascent to the spiritual plane. The story goes like this:[38]

> Once, the great Hasidic leader, Zusya, came to his followers. His eyes were red with tears, and his face was pale with fear.
>
> "Zusya, what's the matter? You look frightened!"
>
> "The other day, I had a vision. In it, I learned the question that the angels will one day ask me about my life."
>
> The followers were puzzled. "Zusya, you are pious. You are scholarly and humble. You have helped so many of us. What question about your life could be so terrifying that you would be frightened to answer it?"
>
> Zusya turned his gaze to heaven. "I have learned that the angels will not ask me, 'Why weren't you a Moses, leading your people out of slavery?'"
>
> His followers persisted. "So, what will they ask you?"
>
> "And I have learned," Zusya sighed, "that the angels will not ask me, 'Why weren't you a Joshua, leading your people into the Promised Land?'"
>
> One of his followers approached Zusya and placed his

> hands on Zusya's shoulders. Looking him in the eyes, the follower demanded, "But what will they ask you?"
>
> "They will say to me, 'Zusya, there was only one thing that no power of heaven or earth could have prevented you from becoming.' They will say, 'Zusya, why weren't you Zusya?'"

This story is meant as a metaphor to express a deeper meaning. If God did have an ultimate question for us, it would not be "Why were you not [fill in the blank]?" but rather "Why were you not *you?*" Are we going to satisfactorily answer such a question for ourselves? Are we going to become and be remembered for that unique person that only we can be? The rest of this book is designed to help you remember—and discover more about—the *you* that you are, at your core essence, at your soul level.

PRACTICE: REMEMBRANCE

We are built to transcend the physical world we exist in. We are hard-wired to remember where we came from and where we are going. It is through remembrance that we are brought to a spiritual life. Remembrance is a meditation that leads to a deeper reality, a new level of knowing, and greater action in the world. It is the conscious effort of reflecting on and listening to our own thoughts, our eternal thoughts that connect us to the heart of the universe.

As remembrance expands our consciousness, our view of the world and our place in it changes. Remembrance is a stepping-stone to spiritual transformation. The world's sacred traditions provide answers to the mysteries of life. At the heart of our quest for mystic understanding are two questions: "Where have we come from?" and "Where are we going?" The mystery of our origin and our destiny is intricately tied to the nature of the soul. As a regular practice, remembrance helps us remain conscious of who we are as sacred beings.

Meditate on the sacred writings that address these mysteries:

"The spirit returns to God who gave it."

"What is unseen is eternal."

"Unto Him shall ye return."

"All things proceed from God and unto to Him they return."

Keeping your focus on the sacred, try to find that "window" in your consciousness where you "can look out into eternity" and see reality as it is: "All is one, united in a single vision of being."

Be thankful for the ability to remember; to remember who you are, where you came from, where you are going, and most of all for remembering God's love that brought you into being. Be grateful for the gift of your soul, your link to the Imperishable.

Take a moment to remember all the gifts you've ever received as often as you can. Take twenty minutes of focused time out of your busy day, each day, to remember all those things that are most important to you, and to let go of the unimportant, so that you remain in touch with your essence. Remember to honor both your joys and your sorrows in your life, because both are what provide your life with its greatest meaning.

Keep up this practice of remembrance regularly. Ask yourself each day these questions:

Am I me?

Am I in my everyday life who I am at the core of my being?

Am I in the process every day of fulfilling my own potential?

And if you ever find yourself answering *no* to any of them, then ask yourself:

What else do I need to be doing to be fully me?

With this regular practice, you won't have worry about answering these questions at the end of your life.

CHAPTER TWO

LIFE IS AN ETERNAL JOURNEY

The worlds expand to him who from aforetime found light to spread the law of life eternal.

—*Rig Veda*, Book 9, Hymn XCIV, 2

Whosoever believeth in Him should not perish, but have eternal life.

—John 3:15

Enter ye therein in Peace and Security; this is a Day of Eternal Life!

— *Qur'an*, 50:34

The highest development of man is his entrance into the divine Kingdom, and the outcome of this human existence is the nucleus and essence of eternal life.

—'Abdu'l-Baha[39]

We need a framework that will help us highlight our moments of truth, our experiences of transcendence, and our transformations. Beyond this, we need a means to address the mysteries of our lives, the mystery of life itself, where we might be going, and how we can understand and relate to the infinite. We need a blueprint, or at least some guideposts, to guide us in discovering who we are at our essence, what we most want to be remembered for, and what our dreams, visions, values, and beliefs are that have sustained us.

There just are not that many guideposts out there for this kind of deep reflection on our lives. The standard theories of human development all look at life within the context of birth (or conception) to death. We are conceived; develop prenatally; are born; develop physically, cognitively, socially, morally, and spiritually over the next eight or so decades; and then die.

The story of human development is incomplete without the recognition of the soul. Rapid increases in global communication over the past half-century have given us greater access to the wisdom of the world's sacred traditions and literature, making it quite clear how vital a holistic view of the human life cycle is. Mystics and poets the world over have long described how consciousness continues on in the eternal soul after death. The most vivid and compelling of these descriptions are founded upon personal experience, some upon ancient indigenous ritual practices.

It is time to ask what our view of human development would look like if we took in the perspective of eternity. What purpose does the soul play in human development? What are the stages of the journey of the soul, not only from birth to death, but also from conception to eternal life?

These are the questions that too often get left out of the process of understanding a life. The guiding question of this chapter is, therefore: How might we see and carry out our own lives differently if we saw life as eternal?

The world's religious traditions, including Native American spiritual traditions, tell us that the road of life is continuous and never-ending. Death is viewed as an integral part of this road; it is understood as the gate to eternal life. As Chief Seattle said, "There is no death, only a change of worlds."[40] The soul's continuing journey in the afterlife gives the path of life even greater meaning and purpose because of the obstacles that are put in our way here as we move closer to the next world.

Psychology goes only so far in describing the theories of human development; the world's religious traditions provide us with much greater insight into the potential of human development.[41] And those spiritual teachings have always been there. What would a Hindu, a Buddhist, a Muslim, or a Baha'i say about our inherent nature, purpose, or destiny? What would they say is latent within us as human beings with a soul?

These are questions that are beyond the scope of mainstream psychology. If we ignore the spiritual, religious, mystical, and multicultural views of what is humanly possible, the stories we will tell of our lives will also be limited; they will not be truly a spiritual legacy, but some other kind of legacy.

Ken Wilber, the leading transpersonal thinker of our time, was the first to look at how the great psychological theories of human development, including those of Sigmund Freud, C. G. Jung, Jean Piaget, Erik Erikson, Lawrence Kohlberg, and Abraham Maslow, connect with the great philosophical and religious–spiritual traditions, particularly with what Hindu and Buddhist traditions tell us about the ascent of consciousness. Wilber's "full spectrum" model of human development is the only model so far that includes the stages of development typically addressed by conventional psychology and the stages of development drawn from the world's great contemplative traditions.

Beyond the highest stages of Western psychological theories are the transpersonal stages, which include the subtle (the seat of archetypes, transcendent insight, and illumination), the causal (samadhi, nirvana, and a universal and formless self, or Atman), and finally, the ultimate (absolute spirit, absolute consciousness, Sri Aurobindo's "supermind," and zen's "one mind").

When conventional stages of human development are taken together with the contemplative approaches of the world's religious traditions, the integration seems to result in a universal, cross-cultural spectrum of human development that shares important similarities across the life cycle.

Yet not even a transpersonal approach offers the perspective that life is an eternal journey. Only the mystical writings of the world's religions do this. There is no other model that focuses on the eternal aspect of our lives, affirms that this can be a real catalyst in determining how far we are capable of growing and evolving in our lives, and offers a blueprint for identifying a pattern to this spiritual development.

THE SOUL IS THE MEDIUM FOR SPIRITUAL GROWTH

Most of the world's sacred traditions, and all mystics, accept some form of the notion that we come from our Creator and will return from where we came.[42] We set off on a quest for reunion in the first place because we became aware of our separation from the source of our being. The mystic's quest for union exists to achieve an experience of unity in a world made up of many dualisms.

The very *raison d être* of the mystic is to ensure the return to the source of our being. The mystic lives in this world with one eye focused here and the other on eternity. As Catherine of Siena, the fourteenth-century Christian mystic saint, put it, "All the way to heaven is heaven."[43] The holistic perspective that both worlds are one distinguishes the mystic from other seekers of personal or spiritual growth and resolves the long-standing body–mind–spirit split.

Because he or she has a dual focus on this world and the other world at the same time, the true mystic is practical. Physical needs are real and spiritual possibilities are also as real. A contemplative attitude toward life, a commitment to discipline, a singleness of purpose, and an undying faith are the qualities that keep mystics from becoming overwhelmed by the formidable forces of the physical world, a realm they know they are only passing through. They are here not only to bring about their own reunion in the next world, but also to help others reunite the disparate worlds here.

Their practicality lies in the power of their commitment when confronted with the continuous sufferings of the temporal world. In practice, the mystics' commitment grows stronger and more intense with every trial faced. This feeds their spirit, renews their vitality, and better prepares them to separate the lasting from the illusory in their journey. Living the mystic life is a practical step that could assist every person to wholeness. The practical approach to this life *and* the afterlife is the way of the soul.

The mystic is also a realist, accepting the invitation of the soul to attain that fullness of life for which we were made. The best, and simplest, definition of a mystic is one who seeks union with Reality, or with the Absolute.[44] The union sought here is through the ultimate consciousness we can attain in opening into a richer and more vital world, thus bringing about a perspective that harmonizes everything there is. The mystic's quest for union exists to bring about a transcendent point of view, to achieve a sense, and experience, of unity in a world made up of many dualities.

The mystic is aware of the tensions that always exist within us all. The mystic acknowledges the cobwebs as well as the beauty of the universe and understands life in relation to eternity, seeking to resolve the inherent tensions by making the two one. Those complacent with the seen world feel no sense of something missing and so "unite" with the known temporal world. It is easier *not* to unite with Reality. But anyone, through some great moment of truth or deep experience of beauty, love, or pain, can be lifted to higher consciousness and become aware of a difference between the temporal and the eternal, and can recognize the interconnectedness—and sacredness—of all things. We remain separated from this understanding until we experience the Reality of things as they are—whole and one.

The practical mystic, knowing that we are restless only at our periphery while still at our center, takes on a discipline in order to remain in touch with the spiritual universe always surrounding us, to participate in it, and to unite with it. The mystic knows also the three levels of existence, the natural, the spiritual, and the Divine, and that as we progress along the mystic way they appear first as three and finally as one.

THE MYSTIC WAY

The eternal journey of coming from and returning to God presents a clearly defined path for the mystic to follow toward that reunion. The mystic way explains the ascent of the soul, or the progress that the soul follows in remembering that it came from God and in moving toward that reunion while still here on Earth.[45] This path defines the process of spiritual transformation as a lifelong oscillating movement from the original state of union to a state of separation and back to union, or from nonduality to duality and back to nonduality.

In psychological terms, this is a process alternating between states of wonder and states of stress, a process of crisis followed by victory. Because this process is meant to move us into and along the sacred realms, it can be seen as a sacred pattern, one that is designed to bring about transformation, a pattern expressed in myth as birth–death—rebirth, and in ritual as separation–transition–incorporation, with the simplest version being muddle followed by resolution.[46]

Mysticism, Evelyn Underhill's classic work on the subject, outlines this journey as a series of five mystic states. First is *awakening* into a consciousness taking us beyond the temporal world, often our first direct experience of the Infinite, which is accompanied by intense feelings of joy and a vision of the Divine in the world, of the eternal, or of unconditional love (or all three at once). This parallels the peak experiences that Abraham Maslow describes and signals that we are reaching the boundary of the psychological realm and entering the spiritual–mystical realm of development.

The second state is *purification*, a willful purging of the imperfections, false desires, and thoughts that are not in harmony with the newly perceived reality. The stark contrast evident here creates experiences of suffering and pain, which cause a series of purifications, each necessary for a remaking of the character.

The third state is *illumination*, a lifting of consciousness from a self-centered to a Creator-centered world, taking us another step closer to the desired union with the Absolute. Here, experience verifies divine presence and brings with it an added level of energy, activity, and often, creative expression.

The fourth state is *the dark night of the soul*, or a symbolic death leading to surrender. This is a swing back, a natural cyclical reaction to the heights of mystic lucidity, that is characterized by overwhelming confusion, helplessness, loss, intellectual impotence, and disharmony that constitutes the final purification of the individual will before, through surrender, merging with the larger will.

Finally, the consummation of the mystic way is *union*, or becoming one with the Absolute Life. Here, although we have to live in the world, we are not of it. We live as much in the eternal realm as in the temporal, as much in the spiritual as in the physical. Being able to live in both worlds at the same time constitutes union with Reality. The two worlds (the eternal and the temporal) have become one; they are unified.

Duality is thus transformed into nonduality. Inner and outer harmony empowers transcendent vitality, bringing forth great deeds. This represents the highest form of consciousness, the deepest, richest level of human development possible, and includes the ability to serve as an ambassador to the Infinite, or a spiritual mentor to others. This is the final "honor for which man has been made," Underhill notes.[47]

THE SEVEN VALLEYS

Many personal testimonies and road maps of the mystic way exist, but perhaps none as eloquent and poetic as Baha'u'llah's *The Seven Valleys*. This mystic treatise, which may be interpreted in many ways, provides divinely inspired insight into the journey of the soul itself and why and how the soul's journey here benefits us in the next world as well.[48]

The essence of *The Seven Valleys* could be understood as a process of learning to see the end in the beginning. The first valley, the Valley of Search, is seen as a preview of the seventh valley, the Valley of True Poverty and Absolute Nothingness, the fullest possible expression of selflessness, culminating in the individual will becoming one with the will of God, the mystic goal as understood metaphorically. Baha'u'llah thus makes it clear that it is through the Prophet that the Divine Will is revealed to humanity.[49]

The Seven Valleys could also be seen as the clearest blueprint for the soul to follow in this lifetime to remember what it once knew of its divine origin and destiny, and to regain its lost knowledge of its essential oneness with the Creator. The interpretation expressed here is but one possibility.

The first valley, the Valley of Search, Baha'u'llah says is preconditioned on leaving all selfish desires behind and becoming detached from all earthly things. The hallmark of this valley is patience, along with severance from everything but God, both requisites for purging the heart of blind imitations, so that the truth of reality can be discovered.

The well-known Persian love story of Majnun, who searches everywhere with undying devotion and hope for his beloved Layli, is used as a metaphor of this mystical quest for reunion. These qualities of the true seeker remind us to never be downhearted, to not falter, and to remain aware that we will be guided, as Baha'u'llah said: "At every step, aid from the Invisible Realm" is present in this entrance into the realm of the spirit.

The second valley, the Valley of Love, describes a state of being so all-consumed with what is sought that all self-awareness, reason, and sense of guidance are lost. Joy and grief, pain and ecstasy, are experienced in succession, along with confusion and paradox. This level of intensity is temporary, but is necessary to move us into a deep and lasting love of truth, and ultimately of God, leading us to a state of selflessness.

This is preparation for the Valley of Knowledge, where we come out of doubt and into certitude, as our inner eyes are opened and the doors of vain imaginings are shut. We recognize providence *in* all things and the inner significance *of* all things. Creation is seen in its perfect form, with justice as an eternal law and grace as ever present. We see that we all come from God, as do all the prophets of God.

This knowledge brings with it a confidence and an unwavering faith, since it is "the cause of spiritual progress and attraction" for the soul in its journey through this world.[50] It is the knowledge that aids our remembrance of who we are, where we have come from, and where we are going. This knowledge is beyond the earthly and the profane. It is a mystic knowledge of the transcendent world, of what is hidden in the design of divine creation.

Clarifying further, Baha'u'llah says this knowledge comes through apprehending "the divine wisdom in the endless Manifestations of God." The meaning in this is that the goal is not merging with God, the Unknowable Essence, but in gaining knowledge of God through his prophets. The Valley of Knowledge is therefore "the last plane of limitation," the extent of human intellectual capacity, beyond which only personal experience of the divine wholeness can carry one further.

The fourth valley, the Valley of Unity, represents a significant transition between the first three and the last three valleys, a bridge between the temporal and eternal realms where "the mysteries of divine creation" are fully beheld. "Unity" refers to the subjective understanding of the divine unity of all created things.[51] The world of the flesh gives way to the world of the spirit, and a heart filled with divine love sees only oneness. Differences are not visible. This valley—the equivalent of the final stage of the mystic way—is most characterized by the spiritual qualities of humility, respect for all creatures, equality, and a more intense desire to experience unity in diversity.

The final three valleys are for the further progress of the soul, when the soul, the mind, and the body function as one, in full preparation for the next world. This signifies a deep personal understanding of one's eternal nature and a desire to fully merge the individual with the collective will. The last three valleys are the highest realms of the soul's development; they describe emotions that come from the soul, yet affect and animate the whole being.

The Valley of Contentment adds a sense of inner peace, which comes from an experiential understanding of God's bounty and grace. Here, the soul sees that "the beauty of the Friend" is in everything, and the mystic notion that "all the way to God is God" takes on new meaning. Tensions and oppositions are more easily resolved; sorrow dissolves into bliss, anguish into joy, and grief and mourning into delight and rapture.

Then, the Valley of Wonderment reveals "at every moment . . . a myriad perfect wisdoms" in the created world. This results in heightened spiritual empowerment and an inner energy, bestowed as an expression of divine abundance. This is felt as a new kind of love, not without reason, as in the Valley of Love, but with deep understanding, appreciation, and astonishment. The joy continues to grow, and the soul becomes "lost in awe at the works of the Lord of Oneness."

The final stage of the soul's ascent is the Valley of True Poverty and Absolute Nothingness. Rather than referring to being poor or not having a thing, this represents, on the allegorical or mystical level, the greatest spiritual wealth possible in the context of eternal life. This valley describes the fullest expression of what is humanly possible in the world when one becomes detached from the things of the world (the temporal things that will pass away) and when one becomes truly selfless (experiences nothingness).

This transformation completes the cycle begun in the Valley of Search with taking leave of the self that desires things for itself. From here on, the soul becomes the chief navigator for the rest of the earthly and eternal journey. Reality, for the soul now, is only that which endures and is everlasting, or the deepest qualities of the human spirit. The primary quality manifest now is the altruistic love given back to the world, in the form of service to humanity.

This deep sense of social action, or social justice, of making a personal contribution to an ever-advancing civilization, comes from an understanding that living in harmony with the divine will is the only way we can most fully develop all of our potentialities, capacities, and abilities. The longest-lasting satisfaction one can experience is the sense of union with creation that comes through service to, and interpersonal relationships with, others. This is precisely how the soul remembers where it came from and how it ascends to its greatest heights in this world.

Not escape from the world, or even union with God, but the fullest possible spiritual development through work in the world is the real goal of the journey of the soul. In the prenatal world, we became fully physically developed in preparation for our birth into this world, but it was not through our own conscious effort. In this physical world, we only come to full spiritual development in preparation for our birth into the eternal world through our own conscious effort. Our spiritual journey through eternal life in the next world is dependent upon our spiritual effort in this world.

LIFE ON EARTH IS A PLATFORM FOR THE ASCENT OF THE SOUL

Our dual physical and spiritual nature can help us considerably when it comes to gaining a perspective on and living our lives in this world. This was well known by the early Greeks (for example, Pythagoras, "Take courage; the human race is divine"). It is also clearly evident in quotes from the world's other religious and mystical traditions (for example, the Lakota, "All life is sacred") and the Hindu ("The Self is hidden in the hearts of all"). [52]

Having been created by Divinity, we are by our very nature also divine, sacred beings. And as such, we are on a journey to reunion. If we remembered this and planned ahead for the next part of our eternal journey, this part of our journey could be much different for us. The single most important factor about the principle of union with Reality, the stages of the mystic way, and *The Seven Valleys* is that they completely alter and literally transform our concept of the human life cycle from one of birth to death to one of conception to eternal life.

The soul has been put on this Earth to seek divine knowledge. We undergo a journey of discovery, and many transformations, in order to remember that we have a divine origin, identity, and destiny. This remembrance fundamentally transforms all our relationships into relationships of authenticity, respect, and compassion.[53]

When we seek something wholeheartedly and with the utmost commitment, we will eventually attain it. This is the practical application of seeing the end in the beginning, of seeing the goal in the search, of seeing reunion in separation, of seeing the end and the beginning as one. The Seven Valleys, in its essence, is a metaphor for the pattern of separation and union, designed to show that—and how—we are always guided, even in our separation and remoteness from God, to our reunion with God.

What is possible is remarkable. Awaiting us is a new type of collective relationship that all human beings can share with each other, based on our common spiritual heritage, our common struggles, and our common destiny, as the human race and as individual human beings born sacred. The challenge is: Are we willing to make our own optimal personal and collective development our priority, or will selfish desires continue to limit us in our development and in the stories we tell of our lives?

One way to envision this is that our life here began as two separate entities coming together: a soul from God becoming connected with matter from the father and mother. Conception, from an eternal perspective, represents our *first birth.* We develop prenatally following a biological blueprint and are then born into this world, which can be seen as our *second birth.*

From this point on, the Earth becomes a soul school, where varying degrees of tension between the two worlds, and between our physical and spiritual beings, coexist. This perpetual dynamic tension plays out in our biological, psychological, and social development until some deep personal experience pops up and perhaps actually takes over or becomes the catalyst for a newly awakened spiritual development.

When the soul finally asserts itself, it becomes more likely that we will have a significant transforming experience, shifting our focus, perhaps for the first time and perhaps for the rest of our lives, to the realm of the spirit, or the eternal. This is also most likely the beginning of our conscious search for reunion.

This transformation of consciousness that leads us further into and keeps us on the path of the journey of the soul is actually what triggers our *third birth* of life, our conscious birth into the spiritual world of oneness, or the realm of unity. This leads us still further into the soul's contentment with and wonderment at our place in the world. As we persist, with patience, and without our ego, we may be able to take that consummate step into living the will of God in our lives. This represents our full preparation for our *fourth birth* of life, which occurs as we enter into the eternal realm upon death and continue on in our return journey to our Source.

The Earth is the world of the body. The eternal realm (which includes our time on this Earth) is the world of the soul. The concept of the human life cycle becomes one of a curve, descending from heaven, passing, with much suffering and travail, through our earthly existence and, at the moment that we call death, begins its ascent back to heaven (see Figure 1).[54] Remembrance of this can become the greatest of spiritual practices. Integrating this understanding into our life stories can connect us with the spiritual heritage that we acquire and can enable us to leave a spiritual legacy that will enrich the lives of others.

Our nine or ten decades of life on Earth, even though we are continuously pulled by both worlds, represent a shadow in the context of eternity, a fleeting day, or a day in school. Our main task on Earth, as seen by the mystic, is to learn to "isolate the eternal from the contingent," to have our focus in this life shift toward eternity, toward the One, and away from the temporal, the many, in order to hasten and ensure our destined reunion. This life can be seen as a platform for the ascent of the soul.[55]

Figure 1: The human life cycle in the context of eternity.

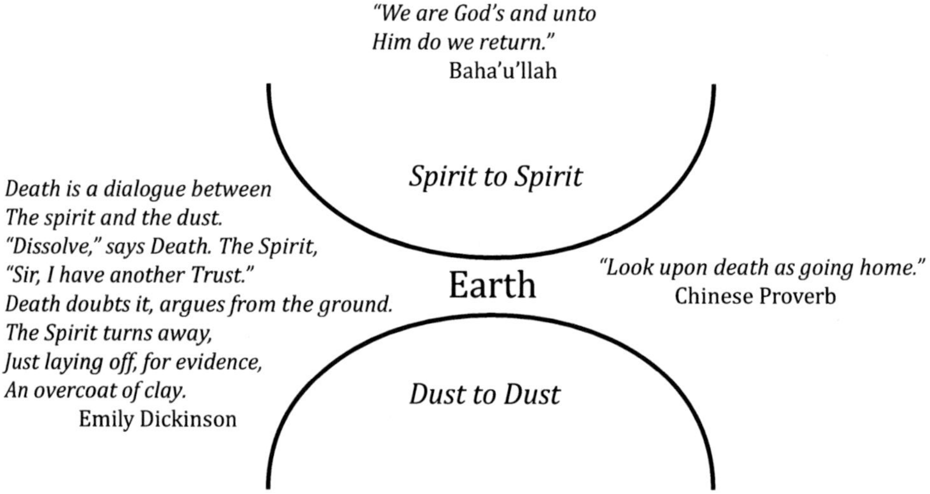

REFLECTION: OUR ETERNAL JOURNEY

Find a quiet space where you can focus your inner thoughts.

Carl Jung says: The telling question of a person's life is whether they are related to the infinite. The world's sacred traditions all start with a similar premise: Birth is not a beginning; death is not an end. The outcome of this life is eternal life.

Take as much time as you need to consciously and deeply reflect on where you stand on this telling question of life. Ask yourself, *Do I truly know, in my heart of hearts, that I am related to the infinite? Do I know that I have eternal life?* Think on these thoughts for as long as you have them.

Think about how your life—and how the story of human development as a whole—would be very different if you, if we, actually lived in the consciousness of our life being an eternal journey, if we really understood and lived as if our soul would continue to exist throughout eternity. Ask, *How would I carry out my life on a daily basis if I actually saw my life as eternal?* Reflect for as long as it takes on the many ways your life might be different if you lived every day in the consciousness of eternal life.

In many traditions, the road of life is seen as continuous and never-ending. Think about what it would be like for you to reach old age and know what you knew when you were born, but realize it for the first time. Reflect on what Chief Seattle might have meant when he said, "There is no death, only a change of worlds."[56]

Imagine what it would be like to be raised from your earliest recognition as a sacred being; to know that *all* things in the created world are sacred; to be treated with honor and respect; to be filled with an abiding joy for the mystery of life; and to never be fearful of the unknown.

Reflect upon the nature and purpose of the soul and its journey. Is the journey of the soul a descent from eternal realms to this earthly plane and then as an ascent from this physical world back to the spiritual, eternal realm, (a journey from and back to God)? Reflect on the stages the soul passes through from *awakening* and *search* to *purification* and *love* to *illumination* and *knowledge* to a *dark night* to *union, contentment, wonderment,* and *nothingness.* Think about how you can relate to these stages. *Can I see my life, past and present, on this Earth as a platform for the ascent of the soul? Can I see my life as preparation for the spiritual life to come, as a "fleeting day" in this soul school?*

After you have reflected for as long as you need to on these thoughts and questions, think further on how living in this awareness every day would not only significantly change your life, but would change your life story. Ask yourself, *In light of the eternal journey I am on, can I see my life story as a sacred story?* Reflect for as long as you need to on the significance of your life story as a sacred story, and write down what this really means to you.

PART II

RE-VISIONING OUR LIVES WITHIN A TIMELESS PATTERN

It is only when man learns to experience himself as the creature of a creator
who made light and darkness, good and evil,
that he becomes aware of his own Self as a paradoxical totality
in which the opposites are linked together as they are in the Godhead.
—Erich Neumann[57]

There is no balance, no system of self-regulation, without opposition.
—C. G. Jung[58]

Ancient, traditional themes appear in the most ordinary circumstances,
and all it takes is an eye for the sacred to see them.
—Thomas Moore[59]

CHAPTER THREE

THE PATTERN OF TRANSFORMATION

Before the beginning of years
There came to the making of man
Time, with a gift of tears;
Grief, with a glass that ran;
Pleasure, with pain for leaven;
Summer, with flowers that fell;
Remembrance, fallen from heaven,
And madness risen from hell;
Strength without hands to smite;
Love that endures for a breath;
Night, the shadow of light,
And life, the shadow of death.
—A. C. Swinburne[60]

To cease moving and no longer be torn by the tensions between opposites
is equivalent to no longer existing in the cosmos . . .
Ultimately, it is the wish to recover this lost unity
that has caused man to think of the opposites as complimentary aspects of a single reality.
—Mircea Eliade[61]

Transformation is the means by which we stay on the life trajectory that we are intended to be on. One way we tell when transformation is about to happen to us is when we consciously experience the tension between opposites as they appear in our lives. Becoming used to these dramatic changes is one of the great challenges of life. Yet there is a way to recognize and welcome such changes.

We know from biology that physical development is governed by the genome, the entire genetic program of the species, and that, through homeostasis, we are designed to maintain a balance between opposing forces in our lives. We also know that through *homeorhesis* we, as developing organisms, persist along the specific pathway of our physical development once we have started out on it, despite the environmental variations or other complications we encounter along the way that might throw us off course.[62] Our biological development is preset to unfold according to an innate blueprint, and we also have an inborn tendency that keeps us on this biological path.

What we don't know, or acknowledge yet, is whether there is a parallel principle governing our psychospiritual development that is similarly designed to keep us on a certain trajectory. So, *is* there an innate blueprint guiding our psychospiritual development? And if there is, what would the implications of having a conscious knowledge of such a pattern of psychospiritual development be? Recognizing our lives unfolding according to such a pattern might show us what purposeful development looked like, or why such a pattern could be seen as sacred, as being the way we were designed to live.

Over 100 years ago, a pattern was identified by Arnold van Gennep, an anthropologist, that can be seen as seen as the foundation for how we understand the process that every life transition follows. He was the first to delineate the organic nature of life cycle transitions in his extensive cross-cultural study of rites of passage, although this pattern had existed in the rituals and ceremonies of many of the world's indigenous cultures for millennia.[63]

He examined hundreds of life-crisis ceremonies in traditional cultures all over the world and found that they all had in common a three-phase pattern consisting of the person's *separation* from the familiar; *transition* to some new learning; and *incorporation*, or return to the group, in which the person had a new status or role. People of traditional communities were very accustomed to seeing their lives within this archetypal framework.

A similar pattern is also found in mythology. There are, in fact, many variations on this ancient, even timeless, pattern, including ritual, myth, mysticism, and more. They all have in common the purpose of assisting us in progressing from the familiar to the unknown, which eventually becomes the known, and then becomes the new familiar, which enables the pattern to repeat itself many times over in the lives of people everywhere.

Socially prescribed, clearly defined rituals were meant to guide people across and between the thresholds of the known and the unknown, and the world's myths were meant to achieve a similar outcome through the use of common motifs. This universality strongly indicates that transitions are the catalyst for all change and growth, and that the process of transformation is organic, structured, and patterned.

Identifying a pattern of transformation in our own lives and incorporating its structure, significance, and meaning into the stories we tell about our lives is our task today, since this pattern illustrates time and again that we continue to maintain a balance between opposing forces in our lives, as in homeostasis, and that we also overcome difficult situations that arise and forge ahead with our growth, as in homeorhesis.

This timeless three-part process of transformation is a juxtaposition of dualities that drives and directs the process of growth while leading to a new and greater form of unity and integration. One version of this pattern, birth–death–rebirth, clearly tells us that we have a natural tendency to find our way to those experiences in life that will lead us to our own renewal and transformation.

Joseph Campbell gives an example of both the pattern and of homeorhesis when he describes the predicament of baby sea turtles. The sea turtle lays her eggs in the sand some 30 feet from the water. Days later, a multitude of tiny turtles emerges and without hesitation starts for the sea. No hunting around. No trial and error. Not a single one goes the wrong way. Meanwhile, a flock of seagulls comes zooming down on them like dive bombers, but they keep on going right on into the water, and they already know how to swim! But as soon as they get there, the fish begin coming at them.[64]

Life is tough, but the existence of this timeless pattern ensures that we will persist in the developmental way we are designed to, despite difficulties, in order to continue to grow. It helps us move from one state of being, or status—even though we may be stuck or comfortable there—to another. And as the pattern completes itself, it can begin all over again. Becoming conscious of the pattern is what enables us to recognize it each new time it comes into our lives, and to become transformed by it. Our stories are blueprints of what is humanly possible.

OPPOSITION IS THE NECESSARY CATALYST FOR CHANGE

As Swinburne's verse shows us, there is an essential dialectic to life, a give and take, a push and pull, an up and down, that is at one moment simple and straightforward and at another moment a core mystery of existence. Each day ends with darkness and begins with light. Fall follows summer. We forget and we remember. This dialectic is with us every day of our lives; it is what makes us whole, nurtures and develops our character, shapes virtues and spiritual qualities, and gives us integrity.

This dialectic determines the most fundamental processes of our lives. A dialectical process governs our growth that balances stability and change and guides us through the basic struggle within each stage of life, as well as across the threshold into the next stage of life.

Through this dialectic, we learn to embrace whatever pain or pleasure comes into our lives. To learn to develop our fullest potential means acknowledging and claiming the fullness of life, the entirety of its wholeness—even, or especially, the unseen, the unknown, the unwanted, the undeveloped, and the unconscious.

This inherent opposition of life is meant to help carry us beyond the known and into unknown realms. It is an essential dialectic whose purpose is to prepare us to become comfortable with the uncomfortable, to help us see the whole from its parts. It exists as the primary catalyst to bring about growth, change, transformation, and evolution in life and, ultimately, to shift our focus from the familiar to the mysterious, from the physical to the spiritual, and from time to eternity.

Life is made up of an ongoing series of dialectic struggles that are meant to move us along the developmental path we were designed to move along. One of the leading theories of human development, Erik Erikson's eight stages of life, is a perfect example of how this dialectic makes up the basic structure of life. Each stage, Erickson says, rests upon a core conflict, or an essential tension, designed to be resolved before we move on to the next stage (for example, from "trust vs. mistrust" to "integrity vs. despair").[65]

This dialectic is as ancient as life itself. It forms the very core of the pattern of transformation. Built in to traditional and indigenous rites of passage and found in the sacred stories of the world's myths and religions, transformation (that which takes us to ever greater levels of being) is the nature—and purpose—of life.

The nature of transformation is destruction (breaking down) and construction (building up), or disintegration and integration. Change and transformation on the physical plane are built in to our makeup, inherent in our personal and collective life.

Transformation is the way we access the higher levels of human existence and the hidden mysteries of life. It is the way we satisfy the insatiable hunger in our souls that draws us ever closer to an eternal realm. Transformation means bringing about an extreme change of form, from one way of being, from one status of life, from one state of being, to an entirely different one. It really means turning one thing into its opposite, turning doubt into certainty, hatred into love, or separation into unity.

Change can accomplish turning one thing into another, too, but it is slow and gradual; transformation is usually more sudden and happens in leaps. A shift in consciousness, a new awareness of something, can happen either as a gradual change or a sudden quantum leap or transformation.[66]

The ever-present polarities that we encounter (north/south, right/left, hot/cold, light/shadow) make the challenges of the dialectic of life ever more apparent; through them we become more aware of the timeless qualities that are sustained and enhanced by the existence of what we think of as opposites. One is actually the helpmate of the other; as each pair of opposites comes into focus, it brings greater recognition and importance to both polarities. Together they make up a powerful and necessary whole.

We all experience some form of suffering, difficulty, disappointment, heartbreak, and sacrifice at various times in our lives, along with times of triumph and breakthrough. Transformation occurs when these opposing forces embrace, when the tension between them merges, but only after these oppositions have forced us to experience the oscillation between their extremes.

Times when the unknown or the unwanted comes into our lives can be seen as having a spiritual purpose. Baha'u'llah, in referring to his own life experience, expresses the practical as well as spiritual meaning of the necessity of opposites, "I sorrow not for the burden of My imprisonment. Neither do I grieve over My abasement, or the tribulation I suffer at the hands of Mine enemies . . . adversity is the oil that feedeth the flame of this Lamp! Such is God's transforming power."[67]

Our lives are defined by moments of crisis, which become moments of truth when these tests and trials are followed by triumphs of the spirit. These core moments facilitate spiritual growth and transformation that involve being able to successfully overcome the inevitable trials that befall us and applying our new strength, resolve, and commitment gained from them to the benefit of others.

This is the fundamental law of opposition in operation. For Jung, opposition is inherent in human nature. He said, "There is no balance, no system of self-regulation, without opposition." The opposites serve regulative as well as growth functions, Jung observed: "Nothing so promotes the growth of consciousness as this inner confrontation of opposites." In fact, consciousness and confrontation of opposites are linked in one of life's primary purposes, Jung believed: "Only here, in life on earth, where opposites clash together, can the general level of consciousness be raised . . . That is probably why earthly life is of such great significance, and why it is that what a human being 'brings over' at the time of death is so important." The "tension of opposites which in their turn seek compensation in unity" brings about the all-important expansion of consciousness.[68]

This principle of opposites colliding and merging to create opportunities for greater growth should be recognized as a spiritual principle that applies equally and universally to all human beings, just as the biological principle of homeorhesis does. The first principle is a blueprint for our spiritual development and the second is a blueprint for our biological development.

THE ARCHETYPE OF TRANSFORMATION

Myth and ritual share a pattern that defines and facilitates the process of transformation. Myth is a teaching story about transformation; ritual is an enactment of transformation. They each reflect a profound truth in depicting transformation as essentially a dialectical process, as do the sacred rituals and texts of the world's religious traditions. The timeless elements that are shared by myth and ritual are known as archetypes and motifs.

According to Jung, archetypes are latent potentialities, or pattern-forming elements, residing in the human psyche—they are the actual "energy-charged," meaning-making content of the collective unconscious. They are part of our vast store of ancestral knowledge about the profound relations between God, man, and the cosmos. They remain unconscious until our own real-life experiences bring them forth into consciousness and make our individual experience part of the universal human experience. Motifs are the smaller timeless elements within an archetype.[69]

When the archetype passes over into consciousness, this is felt as an illumination or a revelation. An archetype itself is the original form of a type of experience from which all other forms of that experience follow and are copied; it is a recurring "mythological component," a common situation, or a universal figure that is part of our inherited humanity.

Examples of archetypes are "the hero's quest," "the battle for deliverance from the mother," and "the night sea journey." Archetypal figures include the Divine Child, the Trickster, and the Wise Old Man. The archetype carries the power to impress, influence, awaken, and therefore transform us.

When we experience an archetype, we are led back to the source of basic human tendencies and connect with the timelessness of the human experience. Though Jung developed the concept of the archetype and made it central to his psychology, he acknowledges that the term has a long history. Jung traces it back to antiquity, linking it to Plato's *eidos* (form), Philo of Alexandria's *imago dei* (image of God) in man, and to Dionysius the Areopagite's "immaterial Archetypes."[70]

Consciously experiencing an archetype in one's life makes the universal personal and the archaic contemporary. This is why an archetype carries within it the potential to bring about a transformation. When contemporary forms of myth and ritual emerge into our lives today, they carry a transformative power. Without them, we face a void, or a spiritual bleakness. Archetypes keep us in the vital, nourishing riverbed through which the water of life has flowed for centuries, digging a deep channel into the soul of our existence.[71] They bring us to life and keep us truly alive because of the dynamic interplay of the inherent oppositions they contain.

Like everything that is psychologically alive, archetypes have the essential attribute of bipolarity. In the same way that a Janus head is turned both forwards and backwards at the same time, an archetype integrates into a meaningful whole all the possibilities of the past and the future. Although Jung believed in the ultimate unity of all existence, he understood that human beings, because of how we think and speak, are bound to categorize things as opposites. This illusory split, however, cannot change the fact that these opposites are facets of the same reality. It is therefore through, and because of, this bipolarity that the archetype carries a "healing function."[72] Archetypes have an organizing influence on our consciousness; their presence is felt as numinous, or of profound spiritual significance.

In myth, the most common and profound archetype is "the hero's quest," a form of the pattern of birth, death, and rebirth, or transformation itself.[73] Joseph Campbell terms this nuclear unit the monomyth, and labels its three parts departure, initiation, return. The process of transformation as a whole consists of this three-part pattern. Yet its most essential form can be understood as a dialectic of opposites that provoke an interaction aimed at, and culminating in, a built-in resolution, or synthesis (as in thesis, antithesis, synthesis), which combines and transcends both opposites.

The process of transformation begins with the separation of the whole into opposites. These are juxtaposed to one another, causing a struggle, conflict, or interaction involving some kind of tension between them, until finally, through a new realization or awareness that clarifies their inherent unity, the opposites are reunited and thus reform, or transform, our makeup and consciousness, moving us further along our lifelong progression toward spirit.

One of the original forms of this archetype of transformation that dramatically expresses the conflict of opposites is the story of Job, who, even in the direst of adversity, finds renewal through faith. This inner dynamic creates the dialectic of light and shadow in all its forms; the conflict is always some expression of lower impulses battling a higher message, with each cycle of the ongoing battle contributing to ever higher levels of moral development, self-actualization, and self-consciousness, culminating ultimately in the union of the self with the will of God.[74]

'Abdu'l-Baha explains the benefits of such suffering: "The mind and spirit of man advance when he is tried by suffering . . . Just as the plow furrows the earth deeply, purifying it of weeds and thistles, so suffering and tribulation free man from the petty affairs of this worldly life until he arrives at a state of complete detachment."[75]

Transformation can be understood as sacred in nature, because it expresses a sacred pattern, is found in the same essential form the world over, is universal, is necessary for spiritual growth and for reaching our spiritual potential, and because it changes us at our deepest levels.

The latent potentialities within archetypes are designed to add meaning and depth to our lives by connecting us to universally human situations, which in turn link us to the whole of humanity. They keep us alive in the moment of their emergence, and they continue to inspire us to seek further understanding of their mysteries. The further along they propel us in this quest, the more do we recognize the illusory nature of their inherent polarities. Archetypes carry a transformative power.

In this physical, temporal world, change is inevitable; transformation is conditional upon our conscious understanding of the intended meaning and purpose of a particular change or transition for us. If the process is stalled or gets stuck in its muddle/chaos phase, the process remains incomplete and transformation can become a necessity, as the only way out of a conflict or a stalemate.

The purpose and goal of the transformational process is not the uncertainty or the chaos of the tension between the opposites, but the synthesis and union of seemingly separate parts that can come when the two parts are able to be seen in a new light as complementary, and as parts of one whole. Recognizing the whole in any situation involving apparent opposites enables the transformation to occur.

The opposition is really there to facilitate the psychospiritual process of death and rebirth in everyday life. This happens many times over the course of our lives, as it is needed for our continued growth. Though there are many forms the process can take, the underlying pattern of what happens is always the same.

Even though change often begins as a threatening possibility, once it is embraced it becomes an exciting opportunity. Experiencing a struggle, being in the uncertainty of a transition, is necessary to reaching a resolution and achieving a greater level of development. The role of opposing forces in our lives is to help us achieve our fullest potential; without them we would fall short. The inherent tensions of life are the scales that balance stability and change, thus bringing about growth.

To experience the dialectic of transformation is the way of this world. It is a divine pattern that we can depend upon. Sacred scriptures indicate how this process of transformation is set in motion with creation and how it is designed to transform the character of human beings from physical to spiritual beings. In Christianity we find, "And we all, who with unveiled faces contemplate the Lord's glory, are being transformed into his image with ever-increasing glory," (2 Corinthians 3:18), a vision signaling a sudden transformational remaking.

In the Baha'i Faith, Baha'u'llah links this type of transformation directly to an experience of opposing forces: "Know ye that trials and tribulations have, from time immemorial, been the lot of the chosen Ones of God . . . Such is God's method carried into effect of old, and such will it remain in the future. Blessed are the steadfastly enduring, they that are patient under ills and hardships."[76] No one escapes the cycle of opposites; they define the nature and process of change and transformation.

Transformation is not an accident. Sometimes gradual, sometimes sudden, progression and evolution are inherent in life. A scientifically demonstrable process of change can be identified in any form of organic life. Transformation is necessary to keep this progress ongoing in the physical world.

As 'Abdu'l-Baha makes clear, "All things are subject to transformation and change, save only the essence of existence itself—since it is constant and immutable." In the temporal realm of the physical world, transformation is necessary and repeated many times over; and in the realm beyond this physical life, the soul continues to experience eternal progress.[77]

A BLUEPRINT FOR SOUL-MAKING

Wholeness is the nature of spiritual Reality. The entire creation remains eternally in the state of oneness and unity. However, from the limited perspective of any smaller part of it, even from this entire earthly realm, everything seems separated from the whole, and even split into endless pairs of dualities, or opposing forces.

Dualities represent division, incompleteness, and temporality. Wholeness is what we are here to strive for in this temporal realm. Beneath the surface of what we see all around us is the deeper unity. It is within our human capabilities to bring together such opposites, to merge them, and thereby restore them to the hidden wholeness they already are. This is how we realize our greatest strength, while transforming ourselves from temporal beings into eternal beings.

Seeing the nature of reality as a whole gives us a blueprint to live by. A blueprint is a detailed plan that a certain sequence of action follows. It is something we can count on to help us see and understand both the parts and the whole, while keeping us focused on the whole. A blueprint is a more definitively detailed pattern, one that we can rely upon even more than a pattern.

Because we live our lives out in the realm of dualities, indigenous, traditional, and spiritual communities have tried to identify and integrate into their community life an experiential process that is designed to help bring about the necessary transformation toward wholeness. The ritual process, the mythological journey of the hero, and the mystic way have all been incorporated into various communities as in-depth expressions of the pattern of transformation in its wholeness. Each of these versions shows us that every transition in life occurs through a process of the clash and merging of opposing forces. We need to be able to see this process as a whole, rather than get lost in or overwhelmed by any of its parts, especially the muddle/chaos/death phase. In fact, seeing only the parts of a process is always what gives us the most trouble. Seeing the end in the beginning is always a big help.

When we look more closely at the pattern of transformation, every version of every sacred story consists of a *beginning,* a *muddle,* and a *resolution.* A muddle is when things don't go smoothly. It is when things involve conflict, chaos, or disorder. Conflict creates the plot of a story.

There could be no plot, or plan of action, intrigue, or drama to the story, without a muddle of some sort. Stories go from order to disorder to order. The resolution is how balance is restored.

The pattern of transformation can be narrowed down even further to the core opposition of *light* and *shadow*. In the world of nature, we can easily notice that "night, the shadow of light," follows each day. This pattern repeats itself to give us a clear picture of the way the world works, and why. The important thing in observing the unfolding of this pattern in nature is that what appears to be decay, shadow, or darkness, is only a moment in an ever-evolving process.

This core opposition is also found in Plato's classic allegory of the cave. As prisoners in a dark underground cavern, the men dwelling there can look only toward the cave wall, where a fire burning behind them casts shadows on the wall above them. This is their reality. But if one of them were able to actually make his way out of the cave and into the sunlight, he would begin to wonder which view is reality, the shadows he is most familiar with or the new light that is so overwhelming. As he gradually notices the shadows of the trees around him, he finally looks upon the sun itself and sees it as the source of the light. This, then, is eventually seen as a new reality. This is also the essence of transformation, as it is completed by the man who finds truth amidst falseness and wants to pass this on to others.[78]

This allegory is another form of the monomyth, the classic journey of the hero who ventures out into the unknown, is transformed there, and must return to those left behind to pass on his new understanding. Both are metaphors of spiritual transformation, in which reality is distinguished from illusion, and light from its shadow, but only after the familiar is let go of and the unknown is experienced.

Spiritual transformation is thus achieved when we are able to consciously move away from the world of illusion, away from the shadows surrounding us in the physical world, and move toward the world of reality, the light that is the source of truth. But this experience is elusive and is extremely difficult to try to pass on to others.

This is made more difficult because we actually do live in the world of shadows. The entire physical world is a shadow of the spiritual world; it contains all that the spiritual world does, and its opposites as well.[79] Plato's allegory of the cave provides a clear juxtaposition, in a real-life setting of light and shadow, of how a physical experience serves as a catalyst in bringing about a new spiritual understanding, or even transformation, through the interaction of the two.

Light and shadow, the core pair of opposites, can be seen as the outline of a blueprint, or an innate pattern our lives are meant to follow, in which each part is designed to be merged with the other to recreate the whole. Light is an ancient symbol that is central to many sacred traditions; it represents the qualities of radiance, sanctity, love, glory, justice, and every spiritual attribute that emanates from divinity.

It is said in the *Bhagavad Gita,* "The Light of Lights He is, in the heart of the Dark shining eternally." In Genesis (1:3–4), "And God said, Let there be light and there was light. And God divided the light from the darkness." In the *Dhammapada,* "Shrouded all about by darkness, will you not then look for light?" In 1 John (1:5), "God is light, and in him there is no darkness at all"; and in the Qur'an (24:35), "God is the light of the heavens and of the earth."

And Baha'u'llah assures us that our share of this light is already within us. "Thou art my lamp and My light is in thee . . . within thee I have placed the essence of My light. Be thou content with it and seek naught else . . . Thou art My light and My light shall never be extinguished, why dost thou dread extinction?" The light is latent within us "as the flame is hidden within the candle and the rays of light are potentially present in the lamp."[80] This is the light that gives us spiritual happiness.

In this world, shadow is most characterized by temporality, limitations, and continual change. We think of this as the shadow world, but it lives within us, too. The entire physical world is as a shadow that can vanish in a moment. Shadow is a long-standing symbol of darkness, ignorance, illusion, the unknown, and also the unconscious. We are in continual interaction with all of these throughout our lives.

C. G. Jung defines his concept of the shadow as all that is within us that we do not know about. Based on a model of opposites, in which we only become conscious of the shadow when a tension arises between what we are familiar with and something that we are not, the shadow helps us become aware of who we are in our totality. Only when we become aware of the shadow qualities within us (for example, anger, a crude act, or a frivolous indulgence; those things we can easily see in others but would want to deny or be ashamed of in ourselves) are we able to see ourselves in our wholeness and put ourselves in a position to make real progress. Understanding the shadow aspects of ourselves is necessary if we are to move forward in our spiritual growth.

The shadow is actually "the paradoxical secret of transformation itself," since "it is only when man learns to experience himself as the creature of a creator who made light and darkness, good and evil, that he becomes aware of his own Self as a paradoxical totality in which the opposites are linked together as they are in the Godhead. Only then—when the creative interrelationship of light and shadow is accepted and lived as the foundation of this world—is life in this world truly possible for man." Thus, acceptance of the shadow "is the first part of a process of transformation in the personality which, whatever else it may include, always involves an enlargement of consciousness."[81]

The real key to the blueprint for soul-making is that both parts of the whole—light *and* shadow—are necessary. With only one of these parts, our perspective and our consciousness would indeed be very limited. Things are most sharply measured or defined by their opposites. And their juxtaposition is striking. Would a rose still be a rose without its thorns? Would the story of Christ be the same without Judas? Would poverty be an injustice without wealth? A conscious life finds meaning in these contrasts, meaning that affects and punctuates our life, and that can even transform us, depending on what we do with our conscious knowledge.[82]

The heart of the transformation process, and the blueprint, is shadow followed by light, or muddle followed by resolution. We have an innate need and capacity to overcome and resolve the difficulties we encounter throughout life. The blueprint and the pattern exist to maintain a balance between opposites and to show that there is an underlying order to such disorder.

When an inner balance, or inner peace, is replaced by an imbalance due to chaos or conflict, this is to remind us of the "essential balance, which is the pivot of the constitution" of our psyche, or soul.[83] Balance is the natural state of existence everyone yearns for and thrives in. This is the soul's reference point. It is our deepest desire to want to find, and maintain, balance in our own lives and in all things.

The divine purpose in the endless pairs of opposites we continually confront in our lives is that they will eventually merge, reestablish the essential balance of life, and transform us in the process. Both the troubles and pleasures that are the heart of this dialectic are necessary to this ultimate balance.

Soul-making has its own beginning, muddle, and resolution, and often many repetitions of these. The muddle/conflict is the plot of our lives, or the challenge, that gives it its direction, purpose, and meaning. The resolution is what we do to meet or overcome this challenge and carry out our purpose. Yet, it requires an effort on our part to give our own story a shape and a form that will convey its meaning to ourselves and to others. We need to become more familiar with this pattern.

The blueprint of beginning–muddle–resolution tells us that we have a natural tendency to find our way to those experiences in life that will lead us to and through our own transformation. A conscious knowledge of the pattern and of what it is meant to bring about in our lives can help us to recognize it each time it comes into our lives; it can also greatly lessen the tension, chaos, and confusion of whatever the muddle is, while reassuring us that there will be a resolution, and that we might benefit by letting go of whatever we thought we might have had to hold on to when it is no longer fulfilling a healthy purpose for us.

This pattern is as close to being timeless and universal as it can be, because it defines and describes:

- **a.** how ritual and everyday transitions take place in a wide variety of cultures (separation, transition, incorporation);
- **b.** how mythic transformations occur (birth, death, rebirth; or departure, initiation, return);
- **c.** how spiritual and mystic growth happen (purification, illumination, union);
- **d.** how traditional and sacred stories are structured (beginning, muddle, resolution).

This is not to say that an inborn blueprint totally predetermines everything that will happen in our lives, any more than the principle of homeorhesis predetermines everything in our biological development.

There are always exceptions to every principle or pattern, and even abnormalities that do occur. What it does say is that our lives are more likely than not to follow this very general pattern to some degree, even with the unique input of each individual's personal experience.

The pattern is experienced by each individual in her or his own unique way. Its existence doesn't mean that we are all alike in every way, but that we are all alike in some ways, and like some others in some ways, and like no others in some way. The blueprint is really like a very general outline, the details of which are filled in by each person's unique circumstances and experiences. It is a universally generic framework shared by all human beings.

The pattern of spiritual transformation—and soul-making—comes down to an oscillating movement, back and forth, between an endless series of polarities, or opposites, also seen as the two worlds of spirit and matter. This oscillation continues until, and even after, we eventually recognize that they are all one, through the flowing together or merging of the dualities into a unity. The way we unite the dualities is through the realm of the spirit, through seeking and understanding the original oneness we began life with and will complete it with. In its essence, this sacred pattern of spiritual growth and transformation can be understood as the basic dialectic of life, often expressed as thesis/antithesis/synthesis.

Our challenge is to see ourselves as sacred. We owe it to ourselves to give our own lives as much respect and reverence as we once gave the lives of the gods and goddesses.

REFLECTION: DEMYSTIFYING TRANSFORMATION

Find a quiet space where you can focus your inner mind on these thoughts.

In this material setting, there is a pattern to life that prepares us for what comes next in our never-ending spiritual journey. Everywhere we turn, we see reflections of a sacred pattern always repeating itself; night and day, spring and fall, endless pairs of opposites ebbing and flowing, one turning into the other, some obviously good and some seemingly bad. *Or are they?*

Somehow the unsolvable becomes resolvable, when pondered with an open heart. The polarity of good and evil is only a polarity when seen from the perspective of either of the parts. As seen from the perspective of the whole, the two are one. The opposing parts complement, balance, and sustain each other, as different sides of the same thing. *Could there be a spiritual purpose to what, from our limited perspective, appears to be bad? Could it all be part of a sacred plan?*

The tension between all polarities is part of the rhythm of nature. The merging of these opposites into one is meant to bring about transformation. In the physical world, the process of breaking down and building up—disintegration and integration—is the nature of life. Transformation—on both the personal and the collective levels—is built in to our makeup. *What does it mean to you to be part of this essential dialectic of life? How does this feel to you?*

In every transition we can experience, this dialectical process has expressed itself as *birth-death-rebirth, or beginning-muddle-resolution.* This is a pattern designed to bring about greater integration, and greater unity. *How have you embraced the change, the pattern, and the conflict and chaos that are necessary to achieve transformation?*

Take as much time as you need to think about these questions:

When has the merging of opposites occurred in my life?

How has the beginning-muddle-resolution blueprint played out in my life?

How can I incorporate its structure, significance, and meaning into my life story?

Write down your insights from this reflection.

____

____

____

CHAPTER FOUR

THE SOUL IS IN THE DEPTHS

Where we had thought to travel outward,
we shall come to the center of our own existence;
where we had thought to be alone, we shall be with all the world.
—Joseph Campbell[84]

Everything is laid out for you. Your path is straight ahead of you.
Sometimes it's invisible but it's there.
You may not know where it is going, but you have to follow that path.
It's the path to the Creator. It's the only path there is.
—Chief Leon Shenandoah[85]

The great sacred stories resound with familiarity, even the ones we hear as children. There is something about them, something within them, that seems to call out to us, as if we have heard this story before. That familiarity lies in the timeless and universal motifs and archetypes that all sacred and traditional stories carry within them. These motifs range from love to betrayal, from loss to quest, from struggle to assistance, and from vulnerability to authority.

It is almost impossible "to be with all the world"; the timeless elements that we all share are what Joseph Campbell refers to as helping us to "be with all the world." What connects us all, and our experiences as human beings, is the vast but limited number of motifs and archetypes that our life experiences can reflect. There is nothing that we can experience that hasn't already been experienced by someone else before us, or that will not be experienced by others after us.

The path Chief Shenandoah speaks of may be the one leading us back to our Creator. It may be invisible, and we may not know where it is leading us, but it is the path along which everything is laid out for us. It is the path where others have already trod, where joy and sorrow, light and shadow, meet, clash, and merge. As many sacred traditions agree, we carry in our makeup common elements, attributes, and qualities that connect who we are in our essence to our Creator. Our very beings, and therefore our actions and experiences, are designed to reflect and express divine or sacred processes, patterns, and experiences.

THE TIMELESS AND THE UNIVERSAL ARE THE PERSONALLY SACRED

We know that our own lives reflect a universal pattern when we grasp a new and deeper meaning by recognizing the similarity that our personal experience of birth, of change and struggle, of leaving home, of overcoming difficulties, and of reconnecting, have with those sacred stories that have guided and inspired humanity forever.

Yet, thinking of almost anything as universal might seem like a bit of a stretch; the image could conjure up sameness, similarity, or uniformity. And any of these might indicate lack of freedom, lack of individuality, or even predestination. But there is another side to universality. Things that we can identify as having similarities also have differences. The reverse is also true. It all depends on the level at which we are viewing that group or individual.

We all have three layers making us who we are: the universal layer makes us like *all* others; the group layer makes us like *some* others; and the unique layer makes us like *no* others. What is important about this distinction is that the universal level connects us deeply to each other, across and beyond any differences that also exist. What we all share as a species is our focus here.

We learn the most about ourselves when we move beyond what we are most familiar with. The unknown is not meant to be scary, but rather to keep us growing. Making the unknown the familiar is how we make the most meaningful connections with others. Connections are what expand our awareness of others and ourselves. It is only when we step out of what is known to us that we come in contact with and become aware of the universal. Our challenge is to be able to distinguish the fleeting from the lasting, the superficial from the meaningful, and the unique from the universal.

We have a natural, innate leaning toward wanting to make sense of our lives, to put everything in its place, and to perhaps resolve some lingering uncertainties. One of the many important reasons for the existence of the normal phenomenon of life review is to help us identify, become conscious of, and be comfortable with the universal aspects of life that have become part of our own lives.

This may be what C. G. Jung struggled with most when asked by those closest to him to write his autobiography. He did so reluctantly, because he was not interested in recalling the usual "outer" events of his life. He was drawn instead to the inner archetypal experiences of his life, since these were what had a lasting impact on him and were what connected him most deeply with the universal.

Once he started writing his autobiography, what Jung referred to as his "personal myth," it became a task imposed on him from within. He could not leave it alone. What was of most importance to Jung was not whether the stories he told were "true," but whether what he told was *his* truth. As he put it, "In the end the only events in my life worth telling are those when the imperishable world irrupted into this transitory one."[86]

Jung's focus on his inner life provides a model for recognizing the universal in our lives. Having spent the bulk of his career explaining the role of archetypes in the lives of others, Jung found that his autobiography was his opportunity to illustrate how the many motifs and archetypes he had written about from the lives of his clients, as well as from the lives of the gods and goddesses of mythology, had also emerged from and actually had dominated his own life as well. Writing his autobiography was practical soul-making.

As it was for Jung, seeing our lives in this universal way puts us in our most vulnerable position, with our innermost thoughts, feelings, and experiences exposed to the world, while at the same time it establishes our strongest position possible on those things in life that we are most familiar with.

Ultimately, this process of soul-making connects us directly to the universal layer of our existence and to a timeless pattern that others have lived before us. This happened in my own life. In my memoir, *Remembering 1969: Searching for the Eternal in Changing Times*, the story of my emerging soul drew me into a universal story, highlighted by the marker events of that historic year, but much more focused on my own inner development. My life had been unfolding fairly unspectacularly, day by day, until one evening when I became fully conscious that my life was deeply linked to a timeless, sacred pattern.[87]

I was walking down 8th Street in New York City, looking in store windows, and a book on mythology caught my eye. I went inside the bookshop and began to page through the book. After awhile, I looked up, and a poster caught my eye. It was announcing a lecture by Joseph Campbell, whose book I was reading.[88] The lecture was that evening and was only a few blocks away. I looked at the clock and found that I had just enough time to walk over there. And that's what I did. It was a spontaneous reaction to my as yet unrecognized moment of truth.

As I sat down in the Great Hall at Cooper Union and began to listen to Campbell's talk, it felt as if he were speaking directly to me, as if I were the only one in the room. He described the mythic journey in a way that made complete sense, because my own experiences confirmed everything he was saying. I realized then and there that I was living the "universal formula" of "departure, initiation, and return."

In brief, "A hero ventures forth from the world of common day into a region of supernatural wonder: fabulous forces are there encountered and a decisive victory is won: the hero comes back from this mysterious adventure with the power to bestow boons on his fellow men."[89] I certainly hadn't seen myself as a hero, and I was still in the initiation, or muddle, phase of my journey at that point.

My "departure" began that summer, sailing on the maiden voyage of the *Clearwater* from New York to Albany with Pete Seeger and his singing crew, trying to fit in as the only nonperforming member of the crew. This was for me a challenge also because it involved a break from my familiar surroundings, which made it like entering a region of supernatural wonder with many new "thresholds" to cross.

My "initiation" occurred that fall and winter, with a retreat inward and backward. I first lived in a cabin in the woods near the river, where I spent many hours in reflection, exploring the world of nature around me and facing my own inconsistencies in light of the wholeness I saw around me. Then that winter I lived as a guest in a Franciscan monastery and encountered a spiritual realm entirely new to me that lead ultimately to renewal and helped to make my experience more complete and whole.

Little did I know, while sitting there that winter's evening listening to Joseph Campbell describe the final part of the pattern, that a few months later I would return to the college I had graduated from three years earlier to teach a course on contemporary folk-rock lyrics as poetry to a group of students, some of whom would be my former classmates. With this series of experiences, my own personal version of crossing the threshold into the timeless realm of a universal pattern would be complete.

What made this whole experience of living a timeless pattern even more meaningful was introducing myself to Joseph Campbell after the talk, telling him how important what he had to say was to me, having him respond in a very warm and sincere way, and having the opportunity to keep in touch with him for a number of years and benefit directly from his concern and guidance. His mentorship enabled the completion of my transformation. I think of responding to the serendipitous experiences of life as a special type of openness, an openness to the mythic life—to soul-making—that leads us further into a deeper understanding of ourselves, our fuller role in life, and our connection to others.

It's like the princess who followed her ball into the pond where it was retrieved by the frog, who later became her prince. When we allow ourselves to be open to a "call," we find ourselves living out universal themes and patterns, almost like being carried along on a conveyor belt to where we are meant to be going. That's the truth I found in my life, and why making sense of our deeper, sacred story is practical soul-making.

KEYS TO PRACTICAL SOUL-MAKING

When we look closely at individual lives expressed in narrative detail, they often identify core transitions that lead to growth and that elucidate in a very powerful way the pattern involved in change and transformation. Every transition, every difficult time in our lives, every noticeable movement toward growth is possible only because of the tension of opposites.

There are always key, critical, and crucial moments in everyone's lives, our response to which determines everything that happens after that. Transformation, the preeminent archetype of all sacred traditions, is a universal expression of how we undergo the deepest, most profound, and longest-lasting form of change possible. It is a divinely inspired process, connecting us to the changeless, to the sacred.

Soul-making, no matter how much struggle or frustration it involves, always awakens noble sentiments within us and spurs us on toward carrying out what we see as our highest purpose. It connects us to our humanness, to what we have in common with others. It becomes a validation that we are all related.

To search through our experience fully and deeply enough so that we arrive at a sense of peace when we complete the quest, to get to the core of our life, to feel our inner harmony, to recognize and acknowledge our gratitude for what life has given us, this is soul-making.

Acting upon this new knowledge of ourselves, and carrying it out the rest of our lives in everything we do, is living in a sacred manner. Here are a few keys for carrying out and accomplishing this vital process.

- *Identify the experiences in your life that others before you have experienced.* These are timeless, archetypal experiences that make up the entire realm of human experience and are therefore shared by all. Jung calls these archetypal experiences "part of the inherited structure of the psyche."[90] They create the framework that makes our lives sacred, mythic, *and* universal, while connecting us to all others.
- *Consciously acknowledge and embrace your experience of personal struggle, ordeal, or quest.* Little by little, as we do this we broaden our scope of consciousness, experience a symbolic "death," attain a greater inner freedom, and then enter into the grace of "rebirth." This is a process that every human being can know firsthand, every time we leave behind an old status, an old image of ourselves, or an old worldview and take on a new view of ourselves or of the world.

- *The more you become familiar with the timeless elements of stories and the sacred pattern they follow, the more you will understand and recognize those same elements in your own life.* This understanding not only gives us a clearer view of our own life, it also helps to make our own life experience feel more special, important, and even sacred. When we can clearly identify the movement from order to disorder and back to order in our lives, along with the resolution of our own conflicts, we have found the universal in the unique and the sacred in the personal. When we do this, we have felt the transformative power of our own experiences and we become consciously aware of the sacred operating in our lives.
- *Identify the times in your life when something timeless, something eternal, broke into your daily existence and transported you to the realm of the sacred.* Such "moments of truth" give us a feeling of being connected to all of life and make us aware of something eternal within us. These moments have the power to set us off on a whole new direction in life and give us the assurance of being protected and guided through unknown realms.[91]
- *Become fully conscious of your life journey and its transformations by recognizing the deep commonalities between personal mythmaking, the mystic way, and soul-making.* The "mystic way," as best expressed in *The Seven Valleys* by Baha'u'llah and reviewed in Chapter 2, consists of the core pattern of purification–illumination–union. The other very effective model for telling your universal life story, or personal myth, is Joseph Campbell's pattern of the monomyth, defined as departure–initiation–return in his classic study of the world's myths, *The Hero with a Thousand Faces.*[92] This three-part pattern parallels exactly the formula represented in rites of passage (separation–transition–incorporation) and has transformation at its core. Each archetype consists of smaller motifs to more clearly delineate the process. For example, motifs within the archetype of Departure are the

call to adventure (leaving home, moving, getting married, etc.); supernatural aid (help from an unexpected source); crossing the first threshold (a new struggle); and the belly of the whale (retreat, or being cut off from the world). This leads to the Initiation archetype, or the road of trials, which includes a death-and-rebirth experience. Then the Return archetype follows, which consists of returning as a new, more responsible, and fully conscious being, living in both the temporal and eternal worlds, always ready for new challenges, and knowing that we are always interdependent with all others.

- *The essence of personal mythmaking, the mystic way, and soul-making is a drama depicting challenge followed by assistance, or crisis followed by victory, which repeats itself many times over in our lives.* The archetypes and motifs that make up this core dialectic express the deepest of human emotions and needs, while giving life some of its most profound meaning. This pattern represents the awakening of the self, the beginning of transformation, the awareness of being guided, approaching the danger with courage, withdrawing and turning inward, purifying the self, discovering and utilizing one's hidden capacities, expanding one's consciousness, dying to the old and being reborn to the new, realizing a serenity and compassion, accepting both joy and sorrow, and remaining assured while giving of oneself freely.
- *Soul-making expresses a pattern in which opposites merge in our lives, creating for us a test of courage and giving us the opportunity to summon from within what is necessary to achieve a transformation of consciousness.* The real story is not the slaying of dragons out there, but of slaying those within us, for that is how we become whole, how we reach our fullest potential, and how we overcome our own challenges to achieve spiritual transformation.
- *When we find ourselves living out this pattern in our lives, we are in the process of soul-making.* This can also be understood as recognizing that there is road map to follow in navigating life's

transitions. This road map describes in detail the journey we embark upon to achieve a transformation of character, of status, and of personality. The process that this transformation follows is timeless and universal. Its pattern is set. It hasn't changed over time. It is very unlikely that it ever will.

- *To live the timeless pattern is to experience the total range of the spiritual life.* The person who has this transformative experience, and is able to share it in some way with others, is living a sacred pattern, at the upper range of human possibility, while involved in the process of soul-making.
- *Soul-making takes you right into the sacred realm of your life.* It helps you explore those elements of your life that have made you authentically you. It gets you in touch with your eternal essence and with everyone else at the same time. It opens you to the timelessness and universality of your story, as it is the story of your life that focuses on the experiences, motifs, and emotions most common to other human beings.
- *Being conscious of the journey the soul makes is knowing you come from an eternal realm, pass through a temporal zone to learn certain timeless lessons, and ultimately return to your eternal home.* The underlying spiritual principle is that the soul comes from God, at birth is separated from the original union it knew with the divine, and spends its life here seeking that lost union. In eloquent metaphorical imagery, Baha'u'llah, in *The Seven Valleys*, captures what seems to be the scope of the soul's journey from making its way through this mortal, material world, with all its distractions, to its arrival at the awareness of God's continued aid and assistance, understanding the sublime purpose we inherit as human beings that have both physical and spiritual aspects. Baha'u'llah extends and carries the mythic journey of the hero and the mystic way to another stage in the evolution of consciousness by clarifying and illuminating the significance of "return" to mean not

> just the physical return home, or even the inner return to wholeness, but now the "return to God" in the sense that the process we undergo in this life of personal spiritual development and transformation leads us toward living in accordance with the will of God.[93]

In what is perhaps the most profound expression of the dialectics of transformation we have, *The Seven Valleys* provides a template for understanding what is achievable through conscious effort, for seeing in the oscillating movement of opposites the possibility of their union, and for recognizing that the resolution of such a procession of opposites in our lives is designed to move us closer to God.

The ultimate expression of the union of opposites in our lives would be living in such a way that our soul and our physical being become as one entity, uniting once and for all the inherent opposites within us and thus uniting ourselves with the will of God. This would mean becoming like hollow reeds to carry this divine will into the world through our direct action with, toward, and for others.

The soul, now master over the physical body it is connected to, becomes a channel of divinity in its ever-increasing commitment to work in the world in service to others for justice, equity, and harmony, working ultimately for the advancement of other souls to achieve their union with divine reality. Its primary goal from here on is to acquire and develop as many of the divine attributes as it can, to the greatest extent possible.

The metaphorical representation of the soul's journey across the realm of temporal opposites, from separation to union, described in *The Seven Valleys*, gives us a clear road map of the process we have to go through in this life, while it serves as a template for understanding and bringing about our deepest spiritual transformation, not through withdrawal from the world, as in some traditions, but through the altruistic love given back to the world, as service to humanity.

What may have seemed like a principle of the mystic life, of interest only to those few who seek the ultimate reunion, becomes a guiding principle for everyone. The living of one's life according to the principle of the essential oneness of all life is not merely a social commitment, or even an act of social justice, as it may be for some, but is really a core spiritual belief designed to direct and guide every aspect of our lives toward the fullest achievement of what is humanly possible.

When we can see our own lives in the framework of the mystic journey of the soul, we recognize that the soul undergoes many challenges in this world and that the many pairs of opposites eventually and ultimately merge into one. We can then apply this template, this dialectical pattern of crisis and victory, to our own life experiences and see our life in terms of its universality.

This essential pattern—an ongoing repetition of a muddle followed by a resolution—is what makes a story a good and memorable story; it has been identified as a pattern consisting of a series "of alternating crises and triumphs," or what has been described as "the principle of light and shadow."[94] Every life consists of some conflict or problem to be solved, whether mythic in stature or not. Whatever our own series of trials looks like, feels like, or does to us, its purpose is to help us regain a lost balance, to help us recognize the oneness in duality, and to even anticipate the resolution in the midst of the challenge. This is the heart of soul-making.

The life stories of spiritual leaders and prophets from every tradition emphasize the archetypal events and feelings that are common to each other and often familiar to us, as well. As with the mythic journey of the hero, our lives, too, are composed of the same timeless, universal, archetypal elements. Every new beginning is signaled by a call to adventure, a quest to set out into an unknown region. Every difficulty is offset and overcome by its opposite force, whether through supernatural aid, guidance from some other external source, or even help from our own internal voice.

All we have to do to give our own lives a mythic, timeless, and universal stature is identify and highlight those moments in our lives when opposition creates conflict, when joy and sorrow embrace and lead to a transformation that remakes us into someone we weren't before. This, too, is soul-making at its essence.

The merging of our dual natures, the physical and the spiritual, is both our goal and destiny. We each have an individual and unique purpose to carry out in this life. As human beings, our challenge is to live in both worlds—the material and the divine—at the same time. For the nine or so decades of our existence in this physical world, our greatest task is to accomplish the spiritual growth that will assist us in the next world, just as was our physical growth the goal in the womb for this world. With the body as "the vehicle of the soul," as 'Abdu'l-Baha states, "the flesh, the senses, and the emotions, are the instruments by which we attain to the understanding of truth. But they must be kept as instruments, and not allowed to become our masters."[95]

There are a few key questions to reflect upon to facilitate soul-making:

- *How is your life unique? How is it universal?*
- *What has been your personal struggle, ordeal, or quest?*
- *What deep personal truth has this led you to?*
- *What do you most want others to know about your life?*
- *What is there about your life that will most connect with the lives of others?*
- *How do you most want to be remembered by others?*

The answers to these questions become the leaven of soul-making.

The key, then, is becoming more and more open to the challenges of life, remembering these times in our lives, recognizing them for what they have contributed to our growth and as the preeminent archetypes and themes of our life. If we were to tell this as our sacred story, it would be one of how we have become whole, how we have realized our potential, and how we have overcome our challenges to achieve transformation.

THREE STEPS OF PRACTICAL SOUL-MAKING

Everything is laid out for us, as Chief Leon Shenandoah noted; sometimes it is invisible but it is there. The path to the Creator is the only path there is. The prophets of God have illumined that path with divine teachings meant to guide us to and successfully across the thresholds in our lives where opposites meet, clash, and ultimately merge. They have highlighted that spiritual blueprint, or sacred pattern, designed to keep us on that path and to bring about the transformations in our lives that will lead us to our destiny. Like the sacred pattern itself, the principles of soul-making, or the process of identifying the dialectics of transformation in our own lives, are based on a three-step process.

The process of soul-making consists of *remembering* who we are at our essence, what our potential is and where our destiny lies; *re-visioning* our life in the context of the timeless pattern that makes up the archetype of transformation; and *reclaiming* a personal spiritual life and the collective spiritual heritage that comes with it to keep us on track to achieve our own ongoing personal transformation, the fulfillment of our potential, and a collective renewal.

REMEMBER

The first step is to remember who we are, where we have come from, and where we are going. This is a preparation stage, leading to knowledge of the awakening of the self to its eternal nature; it concludes with our understanding of our eternal journey and our task in this life in order to achieve our destiny. The important questions for this stage are: Who am I at my essence? What is my essential nature? What am I doing here? Where am I going? How can I fulfill my inner potential? How can I accomplish my purpose on this Earth?

These may sound like complex questions, and on one level they *are*. But on another level, they are all part of the process of remembrance. According to the symbolic Jewish legend "The Angel and the Unborn Soul" (Chapter 1), and many other stories like it from other sacred traditions, the answers to these questions are available within us as part of our original spiritual heritage, which we seem to lose track of at birth. The primary spiritual task of our lives can be seen as the effort to seek (or remember) the knowledge of the divine mysteries we have always had, which also identifies who we are at our essence.

As the mystical journey of the soul in *The Seven Valleys* begins with the Valley of Search, great discipline is required from the beginning of the process. Remembrance is a process that consists of the practice of detachment from the physical world and attachment to spiritual world. This is achieved by the conscious, continual attention to and remembrance of God, which awakens us to an eternal reality and a yearning to immerse ourselves in it as fully as possible.

Knowing that the lives of the prophets mirror that divine reality, we want to learn from and remember them, as well, not only for the spiritual message they bring, but for the ultimate expressions of facing, enduring, and overcoming trials and tribulations that their lives exhibit.

This remembrance moves us along the continuum of familiarity with the universal, archetypal experiences that we also share in. This reminds us of our own spiritual essence and the role that similar timeless motifs will play in our lives. Remembrance of God, of the prophets, and of our own spiritual origin and destiny is the foundation of a practice that creates gratitude, gratefulness, and strength of faith, giving us the knowledge necessary for a deep transformation to begin to unfold.[96] "Only in the remembrance of God can the heart find rest," 'Abdu'l-Baha noted.[97]

RE-VISION

The second step is to *re-vision* our own life experience, the narrative or story that it tells, and especially the portions that represent the sacred pattern of transformation not only in the lives of others, but in our own, as well. This is the volition stage, in which our will integrates our experience of the sacred pattern with our conscious understanding of its meaning and purpose for our lives. Here, we begin to see our lives as having been transformed.

Remembering God, the prophets, the motifs of opposition in the lives of the prophets, and our own nature and destiny, we can begin to transpose the motifs from our own lives onto this pattern, thus making the personal universal.

In this re-visioning, we can recognize that the most important archetypes and motifs in our lives represent a repetition of the basic dialectical pattern of crisis followed by victory, shadow followed by light, or muddle followed by resolution. Each repetition of this dialectic is a variation on the previous one and builds upon the lessons that each earlier experience of the pattern teaches us.

The individual will is of utmost importance here. As Baha'u'llah makes clear, "All that which ye potentially possess can, however, be manifested only as a result of your own volition."[98] This is the inner meaning of merging our will with the will of God. It is only through our own conscious choice and effort that the knowledge we have gained about the pattern of transformation will have an effect on us.

The real goal is conscious awareness of the entire experience of transformation as a whole, so we won't get overwhelmed by the tension and merging of opposites. The ultimate recognition is that the oscillating flow of opposites that occurs over and over throughout life is not only natural, but a necessary aspect of our existence.

RECLAIM

The third step in soul-making is to *reclaim*, embrace, and cultivate our own innate spiritual nature, as well as the entire spiritual heritage that we all share as human beings. This is the action stage, where we solidify and resolve any lingering conflicts or confusion in our lives.

Here we consciously and actively employ the knowledge and understanding we have gained, and we merge this with our will to integrate our recognition of the timeless pattern into our daily lives, so that we can continuously build upon our newly recognized capacities, keeping ourselves on track for the fulfillment of our potential. Our primary virtue here is our spiritual resolve to pursue above all else the person who we know in our heart of hearts we truly are: a fully unified being, one with all.

This step is addressed in more detail in Part III. It requires regular action and discipline, guided by the spiritual truths, principles, and patterns of development identified in the sacred texts of the world's religions. The divine guidance given to humanity by a continuous line of prophets of God has been for the primary purpose of teaching us how to live in the spiritual realm, rather than having materialism and other physical distractions overtake our lives.

Living a spiritual life, with a daily practice and routine that includes remembrance, prayer, meditation, and service, and the clarity, conviction, and commitment that this brings, will enable us to experience the qualities referred to in *The Seven Valleys* beyond the plane of limitations, and to witness "the beauty of the Friend in everything." Contradictions and oppositions will flow together in the understanding that even this physical existence is part of a sacred oneness.

Thus, remembering, re-visioning, and reclaiming (a whole process that consists of knowledge, volition, and action) are needed to carry out, learn from, and continue the transformations that will occur in our lives. With these three steps completed, we have undergone a series of transformations in our life that lead us closer to the spiritual realm and to God.

These three steps may well be experienced as a remarkable narrative of opposites—sorrow and joy, accomplishments and setbacks, struggles and triumphs, beginnings and endings, seeking and finding, helplessness and aid, retreat and renewal, doubt and certitude, illusion and truth, tyranny and justice, matter and spirit, all eventually and inevitably blending in both a discontinuous and continuous ebb and flow of oneness and wholeness, with contrasting elements merging to highlight a powerful and meaningful story. This inspires us to want to share with others what we have found for ourselves, because we have come to know the ultimate aim of the universal mythic journey: "neither release nor ecstasy for oneself, but the wisdom and the power to serve others."[99]

EXERCISE: THE STORY THE SOUL TELLS

Following are two sets of questions designed to help you *remember* who you are and to *re-vision* your own life experiences that have reflected universal motifs. First, choose a block of undisturbed time and find a place for quiet reflection where you can think back to these moments of truth in your life.

When you are ready and comfortable, let your mind come to rest and meditate on these thoughts for a few moments:

> *Letting go is necessary for reaching out.*
>
> *Cleansing is necessary for purification.*
>
> *The unknown becomes the known.*
>
> *Retreat is preparation for emergence.*

Now, following your own path backward to those times in your life when something really changed for you, ask yourself these questions. (You may stay with these questions for as long as you need to and take them at your own pace. Write down, at least in rough note or outline form, what you get from your reflections on these questions. If it feels more appropriate, write your responses to these questions up in narrative story form, as the *shadow/crisis/muddle* part of your soul's story):

1. *Which new phase of my life, which new quest, which time of intense searching, or which new way of seeing things has had the deepest, longest-lasting impact on me? What was leaving the familiar behind like? Did I know where I was headed? Did it ever feel like I couldn't distinguish between guidance and error?*
2. *Did I ever experience being helped by someone or something, being inwardly guided, or receiving aid from an invisible realm when I most needed it? Who or what was it that was guiding me?*
3. *Have I ever felt like I had to summon all my courage to overcome a new challenge, or to cross a new threshold? Did the danger seem to fade away as I faced it?*
4. *Was there ever a time when I felt like I needed to step back, have patience, or withdraw from responsibilities to take care of myself, or reassess where I was and where I was going?*
5. *Did this lead to a time of difficulty for me?*
6. *What was the ordeal, the struggle, or the trial I had to overcome? What was going on externally and internally for me then? What were the inner struggles I was forced to deal with?*

7. *What was it like for me to deal with these difficulties? How did I manage to stay on track? Did I receive support of any kind from others?*
8. *Did I discover any new inner resources or hidden capacities that I didn't know I had? In what ways did my consciousness expand as a result of this challenge?*
9. *Did I find myself feeling cleansed or purified during this process? Did I get a clearer sense during this time of what was to come, or of my own wholeness?*
10. *When I thought I was in control and moving along on my journey, did someone or something try to distract me from my goal?*
11. *Did something seem to challenge the heart of my values, test my faith, or shake the depths of my soul? How did I handle this situation? Did this give me a greater depth of self-knowledge?*
12. *How did my doubt in the face of these challenges turn to clarity? How did my anguish turn to joy? Did an old self fade away and a new self emerge? What was this experience of renewal like for me?*

These questions try to get at the archetypal moments, or universal motifs, in your life that may signal the arrival of destiny and the heart of the transformation process. If there is no muddle, there can be no resolution. It is the coming of the resolution that gives us a picture of wholeness, completeness, and oneness. And this process, with its mighty challenges and struggles, is often repeated many times over in our lives.

* * *

When you are ready, you can move on to the final set of questions.

For the second part of the exercise, think of the times when you have noticed an increased capacity to achieve what you have wanted to, when you felt your life was flowing as it was meant to, or think of what came next after your experience of renewal.

When you are ready and comfortable, let your mind come to rest and meditate on these thoughts for a few moments:

> *Out of crisis comes opportunity.*
>
> *In a drop is hidden the secrets of the sea.*
>
> *What we have been given is ours to give back.*

Now, thinking of those empowered times in your life, ask yourself these questions.

(Again, you may stay with these questions as long as you need to. You may find that using the worksheet below to jot down your rough notes from answering these questions would work better for you. If so, you can then use the worksheet as your notes to write up the narrative version of your soul's story. Your answers to these two sets of questions put together in narrative form will most likely express the *shadow/light, crisis/victory, muddle/resolution* pattern of transformation that is the heart of your sacred story, and which repeats itself many times throughout your life.)

1. *Did my renewal experience or time of empowerment bring a greater sense of responsibility with it? Did I struggle, was I afraid, or did something prevent me from sharing these experiences with others?*
2. *Did my moment of truth seem like I was seeing with the eye of oneness, or feeling a sense of union with all? Has this experience of transformation enabled me to feel rich in spirit? What is this like?*
3. *When I did offer someone something of importance to me, did this help maintain my self-assurance? Have I been able to accept my limitations along with my achievements? What has enabled me to be accepting of whatever has come my way? What are my gifts that I most desire to share with others?*
4. *In what ways have I experienced my full potential being released?*
5. *What is the one thing that I am most wholly and totally committed to?*
6. *How can I use my understanding that one thing carries its own opposite, and that even apparent contradictions illustrate Absolute Unity?*
7. *How can I share my understanding, without expectation, that the greatest wealth possible is complete gratitude for "the things of God's world?" What steps can I take to live more each day in the realm of the spirit, where all is one?*

SPIRITUAL TRANSFORMATION WORKSHEET

Shadow/Crisis/Muddle Motifs & What They Mean	*Light/Victory/Resolution Motifs & What They Mean*

Archetypal Event or Experience:

Personal Meaning:

Archetypal Event or Experience:

Personal Meaning:

Spiritual Transformation Worksheet

Archetypal Event or Experience:

Personal Meaning:

Archetypal Event or Experience:

Personal Meaning:

PART III

RECLAIMING OUR COMMON SPIRITUAL HERITAGE

The lamps are different.
But the Light is the same.
So many garish lamps in the dying brain's lamp shop,
Forget about them.
Concentrate on essence, concentrate on Light.
In lucid bliss, calmly smoking off its own holy fire,
The Light streams toward you from all things,
All people, all possible permutations of good,
evil, thought, passion.
The lamps are different,
But the Light is the same.
One matter, one energy, one Light, one Light-mind,
Endlessly emanating all things.
One turning and burning diamond,
One, one, one.
Ground yourself, strip yourself down,
To blind loving silence.
Stay there, until you see
You are gazing at the Light
With its own ageless eyes.

—Rumi[100]

We have bequeathed to Our heirs
an excellent and priceless heritage.
Earthly treasures We have not bequeathed,
Nor have We added such cares as they entail.
—Baha'u'llah[101]

CHAPTER FIVE

AT OUR DEPTHS WE ARE ALL CONNECTED

The realm of Divinity is an indivisible oneness . . .
The organization of God is one; the evolution of existence is one;
the divine system is one;
whether they be small or great beings, all are subject to one law and system."
—'Abdu'l-Baha[102]

One characteristic of an archetype (the original form of any type of experience, action, or process), especially the archetype of transformation, is that though its form may change in different circumstances or settings, its essence and meaning remain the same, whether it is functioning on the personal or collective level. In fact, the personal is always a reflection of the collective. With but one divine system organizing the entire creation, what is true of the part is also true of the whole.

The archetype of transformation functions in the same way on both the personal level and the collective level. There is but one law of growth, change, and transformation. Great or small, all are subject to this one law, this one process, which characterizes growth and evolution on all levels at the same time.

The essence of transformation, *muddle* followed by *resolution*, or *crisis* followed by *victory*, is the same for the person as it is for society and civilization as a whole. Just as we are each faced with struggles and challenges throughout our personal lives in striving to achieve our fullest potential, and just as these muddles actually strengthen us and move us forward in the long run, so it is for society as a whole.

One of the most commonly understood themes of history is the rise and fall of civilizations. No civilization throughout history has risen to prominence and maintained that level from then on. Here the personal and collective life cycles converge; they each reflect a process of ascent and descent. Change is the inherent nature of life on this Earth. It is both inevitable and necessary. And there is a sequence to all things; the cycle of the seasons reflects the same universal law as does the rise, decline, and renewal of societies.[103]

The most important change is change in consciousness, for this determines movement toward potentiality. Human consciousness is a sacredly endowed capacity for seeing beyond the seen and understanding beyond the understood, yet it is not automatically fulfilled, or even guaranteed. A newborn baby's consciousness is very limited at first. It expands as its development unfolds. We are born capable of transcending our own consciousness by developing a larger and larger awareness of self, society, the mysteries of life, and the universe of which we are part. Society follows a similar pattern of evolving consciousness; each new civilization unfolds, reaches it highest level of maturation, and then begins this process all over again.

TIMELESS UNIVERSAL ARCHETYPES IN THE WORLD'S SACRED TRADITIONS

This divinely inspired process of maturation followed by decline and eventual renewal is as true in the realm of religion as it is for the individual and society. Spiritual and religious consciousness expands along a progressive, eternal continuum, increasing in complexity as our individual and collective development unfolds over time. The underlying characteristic of this process is change, yet it is governed by the Changeless and eternal, making the foundations of the divine religions one.[104]

The world's religions have followed the same pattern as the progressive evolution of consciousness and the rise and fall of civilizations.

A gradual unfolding of consciousness has taken place in the spiritual realm as it has in social and scientific realms. The earliest shamans and spiritual leaders were fascinated by the mysteries of life. They developed a sacred way of being that guided and bonded their communities. Though the mists of ancient history have obscured their names, they too were messengers of God, having brought a divinely inspired message to their people, guiding and transforming their lives for generations, or even for centuries to come. Eventually, the strength and cohesiveness of their common heritage began to wane, and they lost their commitment to their beliefs and values. By this time, another people heard the voice of divinity and their lives were transformed. This birth, death, and renewal cycle has repeated itself throughout many millennia in various locations around the world and is found at the heart of every sacred tradition.

A new civilization, be it civic or religious, flowers and decays, and then another is born, carrying out a sacred process. With each renewal, with each resolution of the muddle, human consciousness makes a significant advance. In a very short span of evolutionary time, the progressive nature of human consciousness, guided and directed by the never-ending outpouring of divine energies, has evolved from a basic frame of reference of the family and the tribe to one of nations and humanity as a whole.

It is difficult to deny that prophets of God such as Krishna, Moses, Zoroaster, Buddha, Jesus, Muhammad, and, most recently, Baha'u'llah have not only impacted the world, but have changed the whole course of human life in the last four thousand years.

It is intriguing that so few prophets have, each in his own time and place, done so much to alter human history and move human consciousness along an ever-advancing continuum. The essential message of religion is constant. This process, this principle, is understood as "the changeless Faith of God, eternal in the past, eternal in the future."[105]

However disillusioning it is to recall what their followers have done in the name of religion, the life story of every world religion is the same. In the worst of conditions, one lone individual emerges, often reluctantly, and speaks with a voice beyond others, claiming to be inspired by God, calling for reform, setting forth a renewal of principles and laws, seeking change, and exemplifying the highest standard of moral and spiritual excellence.

Religion, the original truth revealed by its founders, is a transformative force.[106]

The story of religion also makes it clear that the timeless pattern never goes away. There are always opposing forces at work in the world: forces that would keep things the same and forces that would change things and move things along toward progress. Such is the nature of evolution. From a distance, evolution may appear as an arrow shot across the continuum of time. And even though the prophets of God have been the catalyst for the transformation of societies and of the world, and their creative energies have been picked up and passed on by many others in society, this advancement has never been without a struggle.

Yet as regularly as the ticking of a clock, the cycles of life go on. The universe moves in patterned rhythm, circles, and cycles. History repeats itself. The wheel of time turns and brings us to a new spring every 365 days, and to a new dawn every twenty-four hours. Everything in this world is patterned. There is a spiritual rule that everything abides by.

Why would the phenomenon of religion, or the course of human history itself for that matter, not follow exactly the same principles as the rest of matter and life? Would not this too have to be part of the one ultimate Reality, just as natural, just as orderly, as birth and death, spring and winter, day and night? Rather than being sporadic, accidental, or haphazard, might the unfolding of the world's religions be linked as well to a teleological pattern shaping our evolution?

This is the heart of the Great Mystery that still intrigues us more than anything else. Whether we call the Planner "the One Spirit," "the Infinite Essence," "the Hidden Secret," or "the Greater Presence," there is perhaps no subject on which we reflect more than the subject of divinity and how our consciousness is related to it all.

Our souls mirror divine attributes. Whether we are aware of it or not, this has established a reciprocal relationship with our Creator.[107] We can really only relate to divinity, become like the divine, as we reflect upon and put into action our divine nature. This means returning our love to our Creator, from where it came, and to all of creation. This is the supreme message of all the divinely inspired scriptures.

The story of humanity's evolving consciousness is one with many different vantage points along the way, or different lamps but one light, as Rumi says. The story of religion tells of the greatest single moral and spiritual force in the history of humankind. Despite human-created boundaries, spiritual belief systems have more in common with each other than differences between them.

Whether our particular perspective is from the banks of the Ganges River in ancient India, where followers of Krishna continue their ritual bathing in holy waters to this day; from the precipice of Masada, where the first-century followers of Abraham and Moses vowed in the name of the "One Invisible God" not to succumb to slavery; from the stupas of Sarnath, where Buddha first taught the Eightfold Path and his followers still manicure the lawn using only their hands; from the remote mountains of eastern Iran, where Zoroaster taught his followers that, though this earthly life is a perpetual battleground between two opposing forces, the forces of good would eventually triumph; from any of the twelve gates to the old city of Jerusalem, where followers of Abraham, Christ, and Muhammad converge daily; from the fertile slopes of Mount Carmel, where followers of Baha'u'llah seek the promise of unity; or from the plains of Green Grass, where the Lakota keep the sacred peace pipe brought by the White Buffalo Calf Woman, who taught them seven sacred ceremonies, each of these vantage points is a symbol of the ongoing human quest to bring us all closer to an understanding of the mysteries of life and to our true nature as children of one God.

As Huston Smith acknowledges, "The full story of religion is not rose-colored—often it is crude and barbaric. Wisdom and charity are intermittent, and the net result is profoundly ambiguous. A balanced view of religion would include witch hunts and inquisitions, pogroms and persecution . . ."[108] The full, balanced story of religion needs to cover not only the ups and the downs, the rises and the falls, but also the internal challenges that have existed in every sacred tradition throughout time *and* the external struggles that have pitted one sacred tradition against another, as well. The sacred and the profane have often converged within the boundaries of religion.

Yet from our perspective today, there are many signs that the world is getting smaller, that differences are becoming better understood. Never has it been clearer what the sentiment uttered twenty-five centuries ago by Socrates meant: "I am not an Athenian or a Greek but a citizen of the world."

Since there is still so much conflict and tension in the world, consideration of global affairs makes the variety of religious traditions extremely relevant. Even though religion, with its lofty values, is not a quick fix, still "authentic religion is the clearest opening through which the inexhaustible energies of the cosmos pour into human life."[109]

This essential dialectic of life takes center stage in the story of religion. The first common archetype that comes to mind in looking at the big picture of religion is the battle between good and evil. The world's religions provide much guidance on cultivating the habit of appreciating goodness. Actively seeking the good is precisely what enables us to grow in inner peace and happiness, because the good is a reflection of the Divine operating in the world.

This is where we are naturally drawn anyway. Does our attention, in admiring a rose, go first to the thorns or to the beauty of the petals? The wisdom of the sacred traditions of the world all tell us that it is better to focus on the good than to give any energy to the bad.[110] From Hinduism comes "As the ant collects grains of sugar from among grains of salt, so should you seek the good in the world from among the bad." From Confucianism, "Sift out the good from the many things you see and remember them." And from Christianity, "Whatsoever things are pure, whatsoever things are lovely, whatsoever things are of good, report; if there be any virtue, and if there be any praise, think on these things."[111] The primary purpose of religion is to draw us toward the good of the world, so that we can add to it.

There are two aspects to our nature as human beings, our essential or spiritual nature and our temporal or material nature. In one we approach God, and in the other we live for the world alone. In one we express our divine attributes (such as love, mercy, kindness, and justice) and in the other we express cruelty and injustice. This dual nature gives us the power to do both good and evil; it also means our power for good can predominate and our inclinations to do wrong can be conquered.[112]

The archetype of transformation is also at the center of the story of religion. Its birth–death–rebirth form is common to all sacred traditions in the lives of their prophet-founders. The human life cycle mirrors the natural world with its cycles of growth and decline, seen in the cycles of the sun and the moon, the cycle of the seasons, and the cycle of agricultural fertility. And the lives of the prophets are no different. Whether it is the story of Krishna, Abraham, Moses, Buddha, Zoroaster, Christ, Muhammad, or Baha'u'llah, they all contain the same universal motifs that make up the archetype of transformation, struggle, and near defeat followed by renewal.[113]

These motifs include being separated from one's people, being challenged, being overwhelmed by the forces of evil or darkness, being forced to retreat to a place of safety and deep reflection, and, when everything seems hopeless, winning a great victory and acquiring the means to return and save the world with a message that brings about a new era of justice and hope. Throughout history, this cycle of spiritual renewal has recurred, resulting in the dawning of a new Golden Age.

In Christianity, the central theme is the resurrection of Christ, which is not just about the literal rising from the dead after the crucifixion, but also about a broader symbolic rebirth, renewal, and return, mirroring the familiar cycles in the natural world. This same archetypal theme is found much earlier in the story of Krishna and later in the life of Buddha who, separated from others as he sat under the Bodhi tree, received enlightenment and returned to the world to teach his message.

Rumi has a fanciful yet direct way of pointing out our common spiritual heritage, how we are all guided in our evolution by a common Creator and common principles:[114]

> Every form that you see has its original in the divine world . . . When you came into the world of created beings, a ladder was set before you, so that you might pass out of it. At first you were inanimate, then you became a plant; afterward you were changed into an animal. At last you became human, possessed of knowledge, intelligence, and faith. Next, you will become an angel. Then you will have finished with this world, and your place will be in the heavens. Pass into that mighty deep, so that the one drop, which is yourself, may become a sea.

THE GOAL OF OUR COMMON SPIRITUAL HERITAGE

The endless pairs of opposites we are always faced with seem to have gotten us stuck in the "muddle" phase of our sacred story. If the tension between opposites becomes our sole concern, it can be impossible to see beyond this and envision any resolution to our sacred story. In fact, when the Parliament of the World's Religions convened in 1993, one hundred years after the first such parliament, their declaration did not spare even their own institutions: "Our world is experiencing a fundamental crisis: a crisis in global economy, global ecology, and global politics . . . Time and again we see leaders and members of religions incite aggression, fanaticism, hate, and xenophobia—even inspire and legitimate violent and bloody conflicts. Religion is often misused for purely power-political goals, including war."[115]

Are these the signs of a dying civilization? Or are we living in a time of rebirth? The reality may be that there is no separation between these two times, or phases, of our sacred story. They can both be happening simultaneously, and most likely they are. Indeed, this is a process in which each phase is intricately linked to each other phase.

The view of the parliament did not end with the apparent death pangs we are now experiencing. It affirmed that the basis of a global ethic already exists in a common set of core values found within the teachings of the world's religions. It also acknowledged that humanity is interdependent; each individual depends on the well-being of the whole, and this requires "respect for the community of living beings, for people, animals, and plants, and for the preservation of Earth, the air, water and soil." Thus, "humankind [is] our family," it stated, which means striving "to be kind and generous" to all, with "equal partnership between men and women," and putting "behind us all forms of domination or abuse." This gathering committed themselves to "a culture of non-violence, respect, justice and peace," inviting "all people, whether religious or not, to do the same." [116]

The representatives at the Parliament of the World's Religions see our progression toward this goal very clearly, visualizing the oneness of humanity as a goal built upon a "socially beneficial, peace-fostering, and nature-friendly" global ethic, already common to the religions of the world, which will be brought about through "individual responsibility for all we do."

Spiritual transformation and renewal follow the same process on the social level and the personal level. First, a commitment to resolve the muddle is required; then a further commitment is needed to take whatever action is necessary to accomplish the desired resolution. This is the knowledge–volition–action form of the archetypal pattern, and the desired result is not possible unless these three conditions are met.[117]

What this requires is a transformation of consciousness. The Parliament of the World's Religions start with the principle that "Earth cannot be changed for the better unless we achieve a transformation in the consciousness of individuals and in public life."[118] They acknowledge that the possibilities for transformation have already been glimpsed in areas such as war and peace, economy, and ecology, but "this transformation must also be achieved in the areas of ethics and values."

This means working toward universal consensus on disputed ethical questions; having professions develop up-to-date codes of ethics; and having faith communities formulate their own specific ethic on the biggest questions of life, to make even more specific the already discernable global ethic. They pledge, therefore, "to work for such transformation in individual and collective consciousness, for the awakening of our spiritual powers through reflection, meditation, prayer, or positive thinking."

This further requires shifting our focus from the parts to the whole, since Divinity is one. In looking at the long sweep of history, there is more evidence of biological and cultural evolution as a single creative unfolding process than there is of its opposite.[119]

If we add the world's sacred texts to the evidence of history, we can see a single unfolding process there, as well. In the Hindu view, "He is the one God hidden in all beings . . . watching over all worlds." In the Jewish view, "The Lord is God in heaven above and on the earth beneath; there is no other." In the Christian view, "There is one God and Father of all, who is above all, and through all, and in you all." In the Sufi view, "All this is God. God is all that is," and the Baha'i view, "He, in truth, hath throughout eternity been one in His Essence, one in His attributes, one in His works." Sacred texts are all saying in various ways that the story of Divinity is one story, that all people and all things are of one essence.[120] It is "the Messengers of God Who tell the story of Divinity" in its pure form, since they are the mirrors that reflect the pure essence of "the Sun of Reality."[121]

Shifting our consciousness is a matter of what vantage point we are looking at the reality of creation from. There will be many realities from any limited perspective, but from a perspective of the whole there is only one Reality. To quote 'Abdu'l-Baha: "The Reality of the divine Religions is one, because Reality is one and cannot be two. All the prophets are united in their message, and unshaken. They are like the sun; in different seasons they ascend from different rising points on the horizon."[122]

This is similar to the idea of the great chain of being, as expressed here by Moses de Leon, the thirteenth-century Jewish mystic: "God is unified oneness—one without two, inestimable. Genuine divine existence engenders the existence of all of creation. The sublime, inner essences secretly constitute a chain linking everything from the highest to the lowest . . . There is nothing—not even the tiniest thing—that is not fastened to the links of this chain. Everything . . . is caught in its oneness."[123]

There is a oneness beyond all dualities that the world's religions speak of. The essential message, the common truth, that the sacred traditions of the world have expressed forever, despite apparent contradictions and oppositions, is that there is an underlying harmony and unity to all life. Even the inner life of humanity, which clearly undergoes many cycles of opposition, is founded upon this essential oneness.

Rumi puts it this way: [124]

I know nothing of two worlds,
All I know is the One.
I seek only One,
I know only One,
I find only One,
And I sing of only One.

The mystery of mysteries is that all pairs of opposites flow into each other and create a wholeness that represents completion, oneness, and unity. The essential dialectic of life consists of the flowing of the opposites into one, resulting in a "synthesis which combines and transcends them both." The interplay creates an expansion and transformation of both elements which then form "the uniting symbol." The dialectical process itself is what turns duality into oneness.[125]

This is the archetype of renewal that is echoed throughout the sacred texts of the world's religions, as in the thirteenth-century Hindu saint Jnaneshwar's ode to the union of Shiva and Shakti, the masculine and feminine creative powers, which also creates a "higher synthesis" possible for each of us:[126]

"Embracing each other
they merge into One,
As darkness merges with the light
At the breaking of dawn.
When we discover their Unity
All words and all thoughts
dissolve into silence."

This, then, is the ultimate goal of the dialectical process of spiritual transformation—as well as of the teachings of the spiritual heritage we all share as human beings: a union of opposites into a new and different whole that takes the individual and the society beyond where they were during the tension of the two. The goal of our common spiritual heritage is the resolution of the paradox that reality is both one and many. It is the return of separation to oneness.

In *The Seven Valleys*, as we have seen, the Valley of Unity is where "the veils of plurality" are pierced and we enter "the heaven of singleness." There, with "the wrappings of illusion" stripped from the heart and "the lights of oneness" manifest, we understand for the first time the meaning of the Hadith of Muhammad: "Knowledge is a single point, but the ignorant have multiplied it."[127]

Thus, what we had thought of as opposing forces suddenly become essential helpmates in assisting us to maintain a hidden wholeness. The endless dualities of life ultimately exist only on the physical plane, cleverly camouflaging an eternal oneness that defines the spiritual realm. In the realm of divinity, there is only Absolute Unity.[128]

In the realm of humanity, however, the best we can aim for is unity in diversity; realizing this will move us closer to the promise of world peace, even though dualities will continue to exist. When opposites confront each other, only a created or struggled for unity may be achieved. In this phenomenal world, only when opposites interact, creating a purposeful tension, can progress be made towards the "higher synthesis" of unity in diversity.[129]

Oneness in the realm of God is inherent; it is its singular nature. Oneness in the realm of humanity is intended, part of a divine plan in which, through an evolutionary process, our dual nature has the potential of becoming united, as one will, in service to God and humanity. Unity in diversity is spiritual unity, it transcends and brings together the physical differences and separations into the wholeness that was intended for the human race.

This concept of inherent unity in the divine realm reflected by intended unity in the human realm has important implications on both the individual and collective levels.[130] There is a depth of meaning to the seemingly ubiquitous concept of unity in diversity. It is a way of expressing the principle of the oneness of humanity while honoring all the natural forms of difference that exist within the human family.

Only because humanity struggles with such a multiplicity of identities (ethnicity, skin color, class, ideology, nationality, family, occupation, appearance, age, sexuality, physical ability, height, weight, religion) are there inconsistencies, inequalities, and prejudices, which lead ultimately to racism, genocide, and war.

On the deepest level, only oneness exists, which fosters harmony, peace, and unity. Transcending the limiting identities society gives us and recognizing our eternal, spiritual identity constitutes a transformation in itself. 'Abdu'l-Baha calls upon us to work for the time when "all souls become as one soul, and all hearts as one heart. Let all be set free from the multiple identities that were born of passion and desire, and in the oneness of their love for God find a new way of life."[131]

This is what all the transformations that have ever been experienced have been leading to. The principle of the oneness of humanity represents the higher synthesis of, and the resolution to, all the differences and oppositions that are found in this physical realm.[132] It is the apex of spiritual principles, meant to unite the opposites of the phenomenal world, and it has embedded within it the idea of service to and fellowship with all human beings, founded upon a love for humanity as a whole.

Unity on the collective level is learned and requires commitment, effort, and action. The highest form of remembrance is service to others, or the practice of oneness. This is what is meant by unity in diversity. Achieving this consciousness and carrying it out in our everyday lives is essential for personal and collective transformation, and thus for turning duality into oneness.

THE ONE STORY WE ALL HAVE A PART IN

Humanity's sacred story is ours to remember, to review, and to reclaim as our own. The "priceless heritage" referred to by Baha'u'llah is the uninterrupted, continuous story of the Creator's hand in every era of our history, which has been told and retold in each era by the founders of every great religion and has been lived out by the followers of all the great spiritual traditions. It is the one unfolding story of our oneness, and we all have our role in this story.

In their essence, the scriptures of all religions have given the same message, that humanity is one human family. The Golden Rule and other spiritual values (such as love thy neighbor, honor thy father and mother, or it is more blessed to give than to receive) are all stated in one way or another by every religion. However these common precepts are expressed in whatever spiritual tradition, they are all part and parcel of our common sacred heritage that each of us is an heir to.

The essential beliefs shared by all religions speak loudly to the fact of our differences being only superficial and our similarities deep, that we are all one in spirit, and this is where it matters most. This is what will most enable us to realize our unity while acknowledging and honoring our diversity.[133]

There is a rich and deep well of wisdom constituting the core of our common heritage. Becoming an inheritor of our common spiritual heritage is both an action we can each take and a solution to global conflicts, suffering, and anarchy. This solution needed to move us along to the resolution phase of our sacred story could also be seen as an underlying reason that 144 nations adopted the United Nations "Declaration on the Rights of Indigenous Peoples" in September 2007, affirming "that all peoples contribute to the diversity and richness of civilizations and cultures, which constitute the common heritage of humankind."[134] This triumph for justice and human dignity addressed both individual and collective rights.

It is documents such as this that help eliminate the apparent separation from our spiritual source, and return us to the essence of what the founders of every great religion have taught. If all religions come from one God, all are therefore one. The words of all the prophets get us in touch with our true spiritual nature, reconnect us with our Creator, and assist humanity at the same time.[135]

Rumi expresses the continual unfolding of humanity's sacred story through the messengers of God in this way: [136]

> God does not speak to everyone, just as the kings of this world do not speak to every weaver. They appoint ministers and representatives so that through them people may find the way to them. In the same way God has singled out certain servants so that everyone who seeks Him may find Him within them. All prophets have come for this reason.

Collectively, the prophet-founders of the world's religions have left their sacred teachings and scriptures for all to benefit from. Baha'u'llah, most recently, has bequeathed to humanity the essence of all of these teachings in his volumes of scripture, which illumine life's deepest questions. For example, "The fundamental purpose animating the Faith of God and His Religion is to safeguard the interests and promote the unity of the human race, and to foster the spirit of love and fellowship."[137]

This is the heart of the overflowing "priceless heritage" we all have access to, are the recipients of, and can reclaim as our own. Our individual soul's story can reflect this common spiritual heritage, as well, if we so choose.

Our common spiritual heritage is primarily a system of values, beliefs, and principles for living life here that will better serve us for the life *beyond* this one, or throughout eternity, focusing on the one identity we all share, human beings with a spiritual essence. This represents the deepest and widest of all our identities, and we are not often fully aware of how completely inclusive it is, and how much of a sense of wholeness and unity it provides us with. The important question we are now left with is: Does our global age require a personal identity that must be broadened to a more universal level?

REFLECTION: RECLAIMING OUR SPIRITUAL HERITAGE

Consider this:

> *The lamps are different, but the Light is the same.*
>
> *One matter, one energy, one Light, one Light-mind, endlessly emanating all things.*

Reflect on what this means to you.

Could there be an underlying harmony and unity to all life? Could there be a oneness beyond all apparent dualities of this world? Could the inner life of humanity, though its outer life is caught within the dialectic of life, be founded upon an essential oneness?

Reflect on what it would mean to you to be part of this inherent oneness, to know that beyond the dualities of life there is unity, to know that all the variations are but temporal, and to know that oneness is eternal and changeless.

Could it be that the sacred story of all the world's faith traditions is the same, with only slight variations for different times and places? Could it be that the evolution of human consciousness is directly linked to and dependent upon the sacred revelations of the prophets of God? Could it be that the story of divinity is one uninterrupted, continuous story, and that all people and all things are of one essence?

Reflect on what it would mean to you to be the inheritor of such a priceless heritage, a rich and deep well of wisdom, a common spiritual tradition that has been renewed throughout all of human history, and to which all members of the human race are heirs. Reflect on what it would be like for you to remember, recognize, and claim humanity's entire sacred story as your own.

See if you can; indeed, pause for as long as you need to, and when you have gained some clarity on these questions, write down just the outline of the story of your soul as if it were the story of one of God's most wondrous creatures. Write it as one who not only has experienced its own version of the at-times difficult but clearly necessary universal and sacred story of transformation, but has also come to the recognition that it is one with all the other souls who have ever shared time and space on this Earth, and even with all other forms of life in this endless creation, and that it is an integral part of this remarkable oneness.

CHAPTER SIX

SOUL-MAKING IS PART OF OUR SACRED INHERITANCE

Listen to the reeds as they sway apart;
Hear them speak of lost friends.
At birth, you were cut from your bed,
Crying and grasping in separation.
Everyone listens, knowing your song.

You yearn for others who know your name,
And the words to your lament.
We are all the same, all the same,
Longing to find our way back;
Back to the one, back to the only one.
—Rumi[138]

Every word of every tongue is
Love telling a story to her own ears.
—Fakhruddin Iraqi [139]

The work of remembering who we are, resolving any remaining conflicts, and leaving this for others to learn and benefit from goes back to Robert Butler's pioneering work on the life review. Reflecting upon one's life is a natural part of the process of coming closer to the end of one's life and wanting to be able to have a life-as-a-whole perspective on the life we have lived.[140]

The life review is often a spontaneous event that may go unrecorded, but it is much more useful when it is written down in some form, remembered, and shared with others. There can also be a process of self-evaluation if the life review raises unresolved conflicts up to the conscious level. By re-examining what has happened, it may be more possible than it previously was to come to terms with what may have been long dormant, to reconcile with estranged relatives or friends, to forgive oneself or the other person, and to let go of negative feelings. This process can ultimately give greater meaning to our own life while also giving the gift of a spiritual legacy to others.

Too often a legacy is seen as something tangible, something material, that we have worked hard to achieve and that we leave in a will or as a material product of, or testament to, our lives. But it is, or can be, much more than this. A legacy is, first and foremost, "that desire so profound" to leave behind the story of our soul's journey through this world.[141] This has a very different kind of lasting value.

If we *don't* take control over what we do leave behind, an unintended legacy can result, having an unwanted impact on what people remember about our lives. Simple oversights can cause others to make assumptions about us or draw their own conclusions from what little there may be to go on. This need never be the case. We can be proactive about what people do remember about us.

It would be hard to find a better expression of this desire so profound to review and take control over how one is remembered than what we see in a wildly popular novel and movie of the 1990s. Much more than the controversial story of Francesca and Robert's secret love, *The Bridges of Madison County* tells of the universal need to be remembered for who one really is. Wanting her children to know her on a soul level, Francesca leaves her own thoughts on her life for her children to find after she is gone.

Though it is fiction, *The Bridges of Madison County* is a story of soul-making that affects the next generation. Francesca's daughter and son both have their lives dramatically changed when they absorb what they had learned from the full truth of their mother's life story. They learn not only that she loved another person, with whom she had a relatively brief but life-changing experience, they learn the way *love* defined who she really was. This is what she wanted her children to remember her by.

The deeply human desire to leave behind a story is evident when Francesca's daughter reads from the words her mother left behind for them: "As one gets older, one's fears subside. What becomes more and more important is to be known—known for all that you were during this brief stay. How sad it seems to me to leave this earth without those you love the most ever really knowing who you were . . . It's hard for me to write this to my own children, but I must. There's something here that's too strong, too beautiful, to die with me. And if you are to know who your mother was, all the goods and bads, you need to know what I'm about to say." What she leaves for them is the essence of who she is; she provided her children with deep insights into her soul.[142]

We all want to be remembered for something. At the heart of everyone's deep, personally sacred story is how we have received and given love in our lives. It is about the compassion, the kindness, the courage, and the beauty that has come into our lives and that has flowed from us—yet also remained within us—despite, or because of, all the difficulties and challenges we have endured. It is about what it has felt like to be in the sunlight after having been in the shadow. It is about how we have adjusted our inner life to remain in the light as much as possible.

Just as we needed the knowledge of our ancestors, our descendants will need knowledge of us. Leaving a story of our soul-making as a legacy for them is a practice that keeps strong the chain linking the generations. As the prophets of God bequeath to humanity a priceless heritage, the common, universal wealth of wisdom at the heart of each sacred tradition, we can bequeath to our heirs an individual, personal legacy that tells others who we are and what we want to be remembered for. A material legacy can be as much of a burden as a boon to those who receive it, but a spiritual legacy can only be received and understood as a true gift of the spirit.

REMEMBERING WHO WE ARE AT OUR DEPTHS

Rumi reminds us that we are all the same, longing to find our way back to the only one. And what will we find when we do get there? Iraqi tells us what we will find is already in our own story. "Every word of every tongue is Love telling a story to her own ears." He goes on to add:[143]

Love courses through everything,
No, Love is everything.
How can you say, there is no love,
  When nothing but Love exists?
All that you see has appeared because of Love.
  All shines from Love,
  All pulses with Love,
  All flows from Love—
No, once again, all is Love!

This may be tough to envision. But it brings us back to what may be most important for us to remember: that life is an eternal journey. We have come from God and unto God will we return. That's where the love comes from and that's where it returns, and we along with it.

We're all familiar with the sentiment that love conquers all, which comes from many of the world's sacred traditions. Using hate—the opposite of love—to conquer, or to accomplish anything, only creates or increases tension and conflict, giving rise to even greater conflict and animosity. Love, however, is a unifying force. It is an energy designed to resolve differences by integrating them into a greater whole.

The principle of love as a conquering force is reflected in Jewish scripture, "A soft answer turns away wrath, but a harsh word stirs up anger." Hindu scripture says, "When one cherishes another, the other cherishes the cherisher." Christian scripture says, "Be not overcome of evil, but overcome evil with good." Islamic scripture says, "Repay evil with good and, lo, he between whom and you there was enmity will become your warm friend," as well as in others. Love is what and who we are at our deepest nature; it deserves to be at the heart of our sacred story.[144]

Recognizing love as the source of our core identity helps us remember at the same time that we are souls on an eternal journey. One very vivid illustration of what this all-pervasive love can look like for us, and how it can change our perception of ourselves, was given by Patricia Locke, a Lakota educator and MacArthur Fellow, when she introduced herself at a talk she gave as a Libra Visiting Professor at the University of Southern Maine. She stood in front of her audience, took a step forward, and said: [145]

> I am an old person. I am a grandmother. And I am a keeper of our tradition.

She made a complete 360-degree turnaround in place, and continued on:

> I am a young matron. I am raising my son and daughter. I am teaching them how to be brave, how to be generous, how to be compassionate, how to be respectful, how to be wise, and I am helping to keep alive the traditions of the Lakota.

She made another complete turn around, and continued:

> I am a college student. I am learning the skills that will help me be a warrior in the society. I'm having fun. I'm still learning about the values and the traditions of the Lakota and the Anishinabe.

She turned around once again, and continued:

> I'm a teenager. I'm frivolous. I'm a surfer. I'm a dancer, and I'm kind of foolish.

She turned around again:

> I'm a child, a little girl. They have named me "Tawacin Waste Win." My parents love me. My grandparents love me.

> I sit on my grandfather's knee. I am barely learning about the Sun Dance, about the Sweat Lodge, and it's hard to be quiet.

She turned around another time:

> I'm a spirit child, looking to be born. I wonder where in this world I should go. Who needs me? Where shall I land? Into which family shall I go? I am going to be a sacred being.

And she turned around one last time, and explained,

> And now I am a grandmother again, before you. I did that because I want you to remember the same thing in your lives, that you are all of those segments of your own lives at once, simultaneously, and you can call on all parts of your being to help you though the travails of life. You are still a sacred being, as I am still a sacred being because I am still a child, and I am still a dancer, and a surfer, and a young mother and a young wife, and all of the time all of those parts of me are still with me, and the same is it with you.

She went on to explain further,

> I say that because I want you to know that I know you are sacred. I am not sure you know that. Sometimes in living in the cities and living with today's bombardment with problems, we forget that we are sacred, and we become overburdened and sad, and we lose the joy that we felt when we were children, and when we were teenagers, and when we were young men and women.
>
> I have another reason for asking you to remember all those stages of your life, because if you remember them, then it's easier for us to be friends, to be interrelated, even though we are many different colors in this room.

She explained that looking beyond the external parts of our beings is something we have to do because "in each one of us there is this child, this lovely sacred being. The word for child in the Lakota language is sacred being, *wakan yeja*. That's what our people call children, *wakan yeja*, so you are all *wakan yeja*, and we are all related." She concluded this part of her talk by adding,

> That's what soul-making means to me, that we remember that we are gifts of the Creator, and our souls and our spirits are sacred because they are gifts from the Creator. If we understand this that we must always, all through our lives, try to make ourselves hollow reeds, then that energy that comes through us will help us to be citizens of our families, our communities, and the larger world.

Patricia Locke helps us all remember the most important things in our lives: that we are all sacred beings; that we are all related; that we are in all the stages of our lives simultaneously; that our souls are gifts from the Creator; and that it is the Creator's love for all creation that makes this all possible.

CULTIVATING THE QUALITIES AT THE HEART OF OUR SPIRITUAL HERITAGE

We can only plant seeds we have inherited from our ancestors, grandparents, parents, or society in the garden of our life. These can be seeds of all kinds, both good and bad, as Thich Nhat Hanh notes. They can be seeds of joy, peace, and happiness, as well as seeds of sorrow, anger, and even hatred. What is needed, he says, is the practice of mindful living to help us separate the healthy seeds from the unhealthy seeds.

Planting healthy seeds is like having an antibody to a virus already in our bloodstream; when something unhealthy enters our bloodstream, our body reacts and antibodies come and surround it, take care of it, and transform it. This is also true with psychological seeds, as it is with spiritual seeds. If we plant wholesome, healing seeds, they will overcome the unhealthy seeds. This is why planting only healthy seeds is so crucial to our lives, because what we plant, we cultivate. And if it is healthy seeds we plant, these are antidotes to any unhealthy seeds that might try to gain access in our lives. "To succeed, we need to cultivate a good reserve of refreshing seeds," Thich Nhat Hanh says.[146]

Our spiritual heritage is so rich and vast, but because we live in a world characterized by the clash of opposites, planting only healthy seeds is daunting. Our task could be somewhat simplified if we consciously choose to plant only what we love in the garden of our lives. This is because we become what we love, as is illustrated in various scriptures:[147] "All that we are arises with our thoughts. Speak or act with a pure mind and heart and happiness will follow you" (Buddhism). Or, "Where your treasure is, there will your heart be also" (Christianity). What leads us forward and what shapes our destiny is what we love. We gain courage from what we love. Healthy growth requires removing anything that gets in the way of what we love. But cultivating what we do love is even more important. We cultivate to build the refreshing reserve that always protects us.

Many paths can lead us to the heart of our spiritual heritage, to the ageless wisdom that contains the essential principles, qualities, and attributes for spiritual growth. These are universal. Spiritual truth does not vary, in essence, from one religion to another because, at their origin, there is a common source.

This understanding can be seen in various spiritual traditions: "Many are the paths of men, but they all in the end come to Me" (Hinduism). "In the world there are many different roads, but the destination is the same" (Confucianism). "There are as many ways to God as souls; as many as the breaths of Adam's sons" (Islam).[148]

Our real challenge in living our lives as an expression of who we are at our deepest nature is finding, focusing on, and cultivating the spiritual seeds that have been bequeathed to us by the prophets of God in the scriptures of the world's religions. We each have as part of our potential and responsibility to independently search for this ageless, universal truth; make this what we love most in our lives; and have it be what directs the very essence of our lives and what we choose to live by each and every moment.

The scriptures of all the religions can guide us to get in touch with our true nature and with our Creator. Each tradition has similar principles, values, virtues, and spiritual qualities that can be easily identified from this collective spiritual heritage. Each tradition has similar guidance for taking the steps leading to spiritual growth, and each consists of some kind of regular or consistent practice.

An example of one such spiritual practice is: a) daily prayer with pure-hearted devotion; b) regular reading of the sacred scriptures; c) meditation on the sacred word; d) striving every day to model the standards set forth in the sacred teachings; and e) selfless service. These are ways we can learn about and live the spiritual life; this effort keeps remembrance close to us. This is, most importantly, the kind of spiritual practice that can "entirely transmute our characters and make of us beings entirely unlike our previous selves," because taking these actions will "lay a foundation in your own soul and character which no amount of tests and trials can change or destroy."[149]

MERGING OUR LIFE WITH THE SPIRIT OF OUR TIME

Personal experiences often reach out to us from the center of human experience. They can speak to us in an exhilarating, universal language, assuring us that our own experiences are greater than ourselves. What is at "the center of our own existence" not only connects us to "all the world," as Joseph Campbell has said, but is also the most profound, and therefore the most difficult to explain.[150] Yet this is when we understand that our own experience is greater than ourselves; it even humbles us. With this realization, we may feel as Jung has, that "we are no longer individuals, but the race," and that "the voice of all mankind resounds in us."[151]

One of the primary functions of a sacred story is to provide us with a view *of* the world, paralleling our own experience, while clarifying the meaning of our existence *in* the world. Our own personal sacred story does this as well, by reflecting what is going on collectively around us in the time in which we live. This phenomenon works both ways. Who we are at our deepest nature drives us to want to connect with the guiding force of our time. What balances this out is living into our collective potential as sacred beings in relationship with others.

Jung knew this well and expressed it vividly in his autobiography when he asked himself: In what myth (i.e., sacred story) do we live today? He confronted his own unconscious, asking himself what he had accomplished, and realized that he couldn't satisfactorily answer for himself the question of what myth *he* was living in. It wasn't the Christian myth that he lived by, and he found no answer to the question, "But then what is the myth in which you do live?" He had reached an impasse.[152]

This may also be the foremost question any of us can ask ourselves. If the myth or sacred story that once guided us is no longer guiding us today, what is? This requires knowing what most characterizes the spirit of our time, what the underlying inner truth of our lives is, and whether or not the two match up.

If there is a sacred story of our time, what Jung would call a living myth, it would have to be whatever most clearly guides us, whatever most strikes a chord of resonance within us. What deep truth of the human spirit calls out to us the loudest today? What speaks most strongly to our soul, inspiring us in divine directions? Whatever it is, this is what gives voice to our innermost dreams. What *are* the guiding forces and themes of our time?

The life each of us lives is part of a larger whole unfolding around us. We are all probably already aware of these guiding forces of our time. Since the 1960s especially, it has been well known that a new way of seeing the world began to take shape and move to the forefront of our attention. In the United States, the Civil Rights Movement focused on the inequalities that had been lingering since before the Civil War. In the midst of this struggle for equality came this vision of oneness from Martin Luther King, Jr.:[153]

> Every nation must now develop an overriding loyalty to mankind as a whole in order to preserve the best in their individual societies. This call for a worldwide fellowship that lifts neighborly concern beyond one's tribe, race, class, and nation is in reality a call for an all-embracing and unconditional love for all mankind.

This echoed the vision of Black Elk, the Lakota holy man, whose life story become a rallying cry on and off college campuses during the 1960s, too: "The sacred hoop of my people was one of many hoops that made one circle, wide as daylight and as starlight, and in the center grew one mighty flowering tree to shelter all the children of one mother and one father. And I saw that it was holy."[154]

In the 1970s, anthropologist Margaret Mead, writing on safeguarding diversity, expressed this as "the vision of a human community, who together make up the unity of the human race."[155] She envisioned a global community in which the contributions of each culture are complimentary and there are no outsiders.

In the 1980s, psychologist and psychoanalyst Erik Erikson expanded on his theory of identity development by calling for a future all-human, all-inclusive identity, through which we would recognize—and become—what we already are: one species. When we work toward a wider identity, he said, our narrower identities of ethnic, national, and other origins need not become endangered, but can become fulfilled as we identify with all of mankind.[156]

But by 1969, it had seemed like reality had caught up with the age-old vision. The moonwalk, and the remarkable new photos sent back from the moon, made it possible to view the Earth in a way only previously imagined, as a shimmering globe floating in the heavens with no visible boundaries between us. And we knew from our own experience, with our own eyes, that humanity is one. Our new view of our world—from the moon—confirmed what the great visionaries and prophets of earlier times had told us from their journey to their depths.

It was soon after this, when I made a visit to his home, that Joseph Campbell gave me his book *Creative Mythology*. In the beginning of the book, he offered his reflections on having completed the four-volume *Masks of God:*[157]

> I find that its main result for me has been its confirmation of a thought I have long and faithfully entertained: of the unity of the race of man, not only in its biology but also in its spiritual history, which has everywhere unfolded in the manner of a single symphony, . . . irresistibly advancing to some kind of mighty climax, out of which the next great movement will emerge. And I can see no reason why anyone should suppose that in the future the same motifs

> already heard will not be sounding still—in new relationships indeed, but ever the same motifs.

If "the unity of the race of man" is the primary archetype of the myth, or sacred story, of our time, what are the supporting archetypes that we would have to be able to recognize in the new relationships Campbell alluded to, I wondered? It seemed to me that such secondary archetypes would have to be those that would promote such a collective unity.

Also around this time, I had picked up a pamphlet at a Hudson River sloop festival on the Baha'i Faith, and found that its primary principles—*the oneness of humanity*, and *one source for all religions*—and its supporting principles—*the independent investigation of truth, the equality of women and men, the harmony of science and religion, the elimination of prejudice of all kinds, a spiritual solution to the widening gap between wealth and poverty,* and *universal peace upheld by a world government*—were all built upon unity and paralleled exactly what I had been finding in my own experience. This felt more and more like the spirit of our time, what this age was crying out for.

A few years later, during my master's degree program in counseling, this was confirmed further by what psychologist Rollo May spoke of in a filmed interview about the role of cultural myths in our lives, and about the time in which we now live. He said that we live in a time of a crisis of the spirit, a crisis of personal and collective truth, because the guiding symbols of myth have broken down.

His solution to this crisis of spirit was to live with the myths of the future, with what is going to be the spiritual center of our world to come. But, he added, it is up to each one of us to try to find the myths and symbols that we genuinely believe will become the most important in the future. This is our responsibility to society and to ourselves. May then listed what he considered to be the guiding symbols and archetypes of the new mythology: the symbol of one world; the symbol of interracialism; women's liberation; and an economical system that values the worker.[158]

Because its primary spiritual principles actually predated the now prevailing spirit of the age, I was about as certain as I could be that the Baha'i Faith was the latest expression of a single, evolving sacred story that has continually been renewed throughout time.

Many others, scientists and philosophers alike, share this vision and are doing what they can to make it even more of a reality. The Parliament of the World's Religions' idea of a global ethic is certainly at the forefront of this emerging worldview. With a similar concept, scientist and systems theorist Ervin Laszlo sees a planetary consciousness emerging that is characterized by "knowing, as well as feeling, the vital interdependence and essential oneness of humankind" as well as "the conscious adoption of the ethic and the ethos that this entails." He sees the evolution of planetary consciousness as "the basic imperative of human survival on this planet."[159]

At the heart of the consciousness that we live by is the identity that we carry within us. Both a global ethic and a planetary consciousness imply a broader, more universal identity than we may have previously known or been comfortable with. James Redfield and Michael Murphy, the authors of *God and the Evolving Universe,* call our fullest identity possible our "transcendent identity." The forces of our time carry the seed of "a greater integration" that is "pressing to be born in us." Our personal identity has the potential to expand outward from us and take in larger and larger circles of others around us. Redfield and Murphy acknowledge what the Parliament of the World's Religions had said, that saints and sages since antiquity have claimed that we can realize an identity beyond our personal history. Whether we refer to this transcendent identity as *Atman* (from the Hindu Upanishads), "the soul at one with God," or as oneness, when it is experienced we feel as though we have discovered who we really are.[160]

And when we remember that we are essentially a soul on an eternal journey, our identity, viewed from this perspective, can shift dramatically and quickly. When I reflect on this from my eternal perspective, no longer are any of my narrower physical, biological, or social time-limited identities all of what define me. I am free to take on the identity of the soul; this *me* knows that I am already in communion with the Divine, with every other living creature, and with the entire universe around me. This is the identity that shifts our viewpoint from the fragmented parts to the entire whole, and at the same time shifts our consciousness from one of duality to oneness.

This leads further, and naturally, to taking on the identity of a world citizen. An important piece of the global ethic and the "sea change in human consciousness" that is underway now is an emerging consciousness of such a world citizenship. As we process the transformations now taking place on the shrinking planet we inhabit—mass travel on an international scale, enormous migrations, greater in the last century and a half than ever before, and millions of refugees fleeing from persecution—it is evident that consciousness of world citizenship is becoming more and more a reality, as well as a necessity.[161]

Amid these changes and the suffering all this turmoil has caused, we have also witnessed the progressive integration of the world's peoples into the citizenry of a single global homeland. As a result, people everywhere are now exposed to the cultures and norms of others about whom their forefathers knew little or nothing. This has in turn opened up a search for meaning on a scale not known before.

Being a citizen of the world first and foremost means having a consciousness, a frame of mind, a way of seeing and acting in the world that involves adopting a set of perspectives, approaches, and values that make the whole a greater priority than any of its parts. It means not being limited any one of our identities, whether they be familial, ethnic, or national. It would free us of a restrictive nationalistic perspective and enable us to see and know the entire world as a whole. We would be able to see and take in views, values, beliefs, and other ways of life that may be new to us and different from what we are most used to while recognizing and appreciating cultural and other differences, being comfortable with the diversity of viewpoints that exist in the world, and starting off with a global perspective on issues.

A world citizen has a personal commitment to a unifying set of values that promote equitable and sustainable development well into the future. This is built upon a deep, practical understanding of the interconnectedness of the nations and peoples of the world. This widens our allegiance to humanity as the primary reference group, rather than any one ethnic, social, or nationality group, and results in a love of humanity as a whole. The entire world becomes our home and all humanity our family. A profound sense of responsibility for the fate of the planet and for the welfare of the entire human family comes with this.

How we live out our lives as citizens of the world becomes the context for our souls' journey, and for the story we tell about our lives. Soul-making is as much about our state of consciousness—and what we do in the world with that—as it is about the things that happen to us. How we think about and visualize our place in the world tells us as much about who we really are as anything else.

Peter Russell has said the emergence of a "global brain" is as different from consciousness as consciousness is from life, as life is from matter.[162] Robert Wright puts it this way: "The fitful but relentless tendency of invisible social brains to hook up with each other, and eventually submerge themselves into a larger brain, is a central theme of history. The culmination of that process—the construction of a single, planetary brain—is what we are witnessing today, with all its disruptive yet ultimately integrative effects."[163]

If global consciousness most characterizes the spirit of our time, as many leading thinkers say, we have some big questions to ask ourselves about who we really are and how we want to be remembered by others in the decades, even centuries, to come.

We need to be able to answer the really important questions of our times: What am I certain of? What most characterizes the future I want for my descendants and myself? What would help bring about a more equitable balance between the feminine and masculine influences in society? What would it mean if science and religion really were in harmony? How can economic equity in the world be achieved? Can I even live my life without having some sense of being a citizen of the world?

The answers to these most pressing questions are within you, in your own experience, within the truth that makes up your life. To know the questions is to be on a quest. To be on a quest is to be open, to be ready. Our own questions help us make sense of our own experience. Our own autobiographical truth has a great deal to teach us about our relationship with others and the world we live in.

Robert Johnson suggests that "the Great Quest" is no longer that of the conquering (masculine) hero, who defends his territory, his principles, his woman, and his rights, but is rather that of the embracing hero/ine, who finds the right place for each relationship in life, who nurtures, protects, and comforts so growth can take place in a field of love and wholeness. Is the heroic task of our time "to learn to love—if our planet and our civilization are to survive much beyond our present era?"[164]

As we come to understand the role and purpose of archetypes, mythic themes, and the sacred pattern in our lives, a deep appreciation for the commonalities we share grows. As we become more open to other people, their experiences, and their views, we see that differences are only skin deep, that we really are more alike than we thought.

As cultural evolution has progressed, those living in each era of history have been intertwined with greater and greater numbers of people in regions that are farther and farther away from wherever they are in the world. And with this expansion in every physical and social realm has come an expansion in personal and collective consciousness as well.

All of this makes the life journey each of us is living in this transformational time extremely vital to the whole. If the sacred story in which we are living today is founded upon planetary transformation, leading us away from ego-centeredness and to a unified field of shared awareness, how are our souls to be made? How are we to come to know our divine identity? How, but from a consciousness of the struggles, conflicts, chaos, and challenges of the time in which we find ourselves now living.

The raw materials of our own soul-making reveals the common threads that we share with all of humanity. Our deeper story tells a familiar story. The part is a reflection of the whole. The personal mirrors the collective. The collective validates the personal. The two together tell one story. The stories we tell of our lives help us realize our inherent and intended unity as one human family.

If it is as true for you as it is for many people today that the spirit of our time is captured by the consciousness of the oneness of humanity, how would this be reflected in your own soul-making? Could it be that all the previous sacred traditions have been preparing us to realize in our time of complexity and interconnectedness that, in the words of Baha'u'llah, "The earth is but one country and mankind its citizens?" If we can find in our own experience any aspect of this timeless, universal spiritual heritage, we will have found our own soul-making to be in harmony with the spirit of our time.

If we remember who we are at our essence, what our true nature is, that we are souls on an eternal journey, and that we are *all* on this same mystic journey, we will have connected with the core of creation.

EXERCISE: SOUL-MAKING IS FOR THE BENEFIT OF ALL

It is most likely clear to you now that you have some role, however large or small, in the grand scheme of things. If you hadn't before, you probably understand now that you have something to offer others.

The mystic journey leads directly to the path of service. We may not even recognize it as such until we are conscious of being an integral part of a larger whole—and until we incorporate this into our being.

The mystic journey of soul-making is therefore by no means solitary, but one meant to be shared by everyone. It is not just for our own benefit, but also for the advancement of civilization. We choose this path, by exercising our own will, to cultivate the innate qualities of the soul that are the heart of our common spiritual heritage.

Through our soul-making, we have become a clear channel for the expression of divine attributes, with an ever-increasing commitment to work in the world for justice, equity, and harmony, ultimately having the potential to influence other souls.

Soul-making has also shown us what we most profoundly desire to leave behind when we are gone, and how we will be remembered.

Now, to pull all of our expanding awareness together, reflect on these questions:

> *What is most important in my life that affects the lives of others, too? What is the one value or belief I want to live my life for?*
>
> *How has my soul-making expressed my own personal truth, as well as some part of the collective truth of us all?*
>
> *What is my vision of the collective future of humanity? What role do I want to play in this vision? In what ways does my own experience reflect what I see unfolding in the world around me? In other words, what's the big picture and how do I fit in? What resources do I feel are at my disposal to assist me in carrying this out?*
>
> *What in my life experience has given me the wisdom and power to serve others? What in my journey could become a guiding principle for others?*
>
> *What in my journey has made me want to contribute even more personally to social justice and the betterment of the world? How do I most want to express my altruistic love in the world?*
>
> *What do I consider to be the greatest collective truth of our time? How does my core being connect to this? What are the strong threads that make up my life, ones that I also share with all of humanity? What would I most want to give, or say, to the generations to come after me?*

Meditate on these questions for a while. After you have savored the thoughts that come to your mind, turn to the outline of your soul's story that you wrote at the end of the last chapter, and flesh out these notes into a flowing, detailed narrative that expresses your experience of soul-making, with all its difficulties and challenges, twists and turns, and spiritual lessons gained. This is the heart of the story of your eternal journey, linking you to and fitting you into the whole; it is deeply connected to the story every other soul would tell.

ACKNOWLEDGMENTS

This is one of those books that has been a long time in the making, shifting focus somewhat and evolving over many years of writing about how we can understand and record our lives from a variety of vantage points and thinking even more about what all of this really means in the grand scheme of things. There are therefore many people all along the way that I am indebted to for contributing in one way or another to this current expression of my thinking on this topic. I could acknowledge all those that I did in my earlier books and it would be very appropriate to mention them again here, as this is a deeper continuation and expansion of what has come before this.

My earliest mentors, who will always remain my pivotal influences on anything to do with living a meaningful, patterned, and purposeful life, are Pete Seeger and Joseph Campbell. They came into my life in my mid-twenties and their graciousness and openness to be guides came at the perfect time. I learned from their actions as much as from what they said in their written or spoken words.

I mostly want to thank all of my students over the past couple of decades who have allowed me to bounce the idea of an inborn pattern, blueprint, or general structure for our spiritual development off them so I could see if it made as much sense to them as it has for me. Their reactions have helped me see its power in a more pronounced way, and confirm its universality, even across genders.

Among those who have been most helpful and inspiring to me in this work in various ways at different points are Patricia Locke, Thomas Moore, Sam Keen, Michael Dowd, Brian Hilliard, Stan Krippner, Phil Cousineau, and Wayne Muller.

I'd especially like to thank Ross Woodman for his support, understanding, and recognition of our common experience and commitment, even while deeply involved in the care of his wife, Marion. For their willingness to offer assistance and insights, I am grateful to Sally Dedecker, Robert Stockman, Martha Schweitz, and Phyllis Ring, as I am to Pam Dyer, Kristen Lombard, Mary Fogg.

For her expert editorial handling of the manuscript, I want to thank Isabel Stein. For taking time out of their busy schedules to read and comment on the manuscript, I extend my gratitude to Jean Houston, Stephen Larsen, and Gregg Lavoy.

Alex Dake and Katherine Mason at Cosimo Books have been a pleasure to work with, and I thank them for their commitment to take this project on and their sustained guidance and support in seeing the process through.

And most of all, my deepest appreciation and lasting gratitude goes to Cynthia, for always being there, and for reading what I write with such understanding, detachment, honesty, and wisdom.

NOTES

1 Rumi, "Your Worth," Mathnawi (III, 2652–2654), in The Rumi Collection, Kabir Helminski, ed. (Boston: Shambhala, 1998), p. 2.

2 Confucius, *The Great Learning, A Sourcebook in Chinese Philosophy.* Wing-tsit Chan, trans. (Princeton, N. J.: Princeton University Press, 1963), pp. 86–87.

3 "The Angel and the Unborn Soul," in Louis Ginzberg, ed., *The Legends of the Jews, Volume 1, From the Creation to Jacob.* Henrietta Szold, trans. (Baltimore: Johns Hopkins University Press, 1998).

4 Plato, *The Republic, Book X* (New York: Oxford University Press, World Classics, 2008).

5 John Keats, *Selected Letters* (New York: Oxford University Press, World Classics, 2009), p. 232.

6 C. J. Jung, "Stages of Life," *in Modern Man in Search of a Soul* (New York: Harcourt Brace Jovanovich, 1933), p. 109.

INTRODUCTION

7 John Keats, *Selected Letters.* (New York: Oxford University Press, World Classics, 2009), p. 232.

8 Thomas Moore, *Soul Mates* (New York: Harper Perennial, 1994), p. 249.

9 Marion Woodman, *Coming Home to Myself* (San Francisco: Conari Press, 2001), p. 247. *Conscious Femininity* (Toronto: Inner City Books, 1993), p. 71.

10 John Keats, *Selected Letters*, 232–233.

11 C. G. Jung, *Memories, Dreams, Reflections.* (New York: Vintage, 1963, pp. 3–5.

12 James Hillman, *The Soul's Code: In Search of Character and Calling* (New York: Random House, 1996), pp. 3–14.

13 James Hillman, *The Force of Character* (New York: Ballantine Books, 1999), p. 182

14 *C. G. Jung, Alchemical Studies (The Collected Works of C. G. Jung Vol. 13)*, R. F. C. Hull, trans., Bollingen Series XX (Princeton, N. J.: Princeton University Press, 1983), p. 50; James Hillman, *The Force of Character*, pp. 88–93, 112.

15 James Hillman, *The Force of Character*, pp. 91–93.

16 Thomas Moore, *Dark Nights of the Soul* (New York: Gotham Books/ Penguin, 2004).

CHAPTER 1: Remembrance Is a Spiritual Practice

17 *Mundaka Upanishad* 2, 1: 1 Max Muller, trans. http://www.sacred-texts.com/hin/sbe15/sbe15018.htm

18 William Wordsworth, "Ode: Intimations of Immortality from Recollections of Early Childhood," in Arthur Quiller-Couch, ed., *The Oxford Book of English Verse*, 1250–1900 (Oxford: Clarendon, 1919).

19 Dan Cohn-Sherbok, *Jewish Mysticism: An Anthology* (Oxford: Oneworld, 1995), pp. 173–76; Geoffrey Parrinder, *Mysticism in the World's Religion* (Oxford: Oneworld, 1995), pp. 112–13.

20 Bede Griffiths, *Return to the Center* (Springfield, IL: Templegate, 1977).

21 in D. L. Carmody and J. T. Carmody, *Mysticism: Holiness East and West* (New York: Oxford University Press, 1966), p. 260.

22 Baha'u'llah, *The Kitab-i-Aqdas* (Haifa: Baha'i World Center, 1992), p. 72; Shoghi Effendi, *Directives from the Guardian* (New Delhi: Baha'i Publishing Trust, 1973), p. 86.

23 "The Angel and the Unborn Soul" in Louis Ginzberg, ed., *The Legends of the Jews, Volume 1, From the Creation to Jacob.* Henrietta Szold, trans. (Baltimore: Johns Hopkins University Press, 1998).

24 Robert Frager, *Heart, Self, & Soul: The Sufi Psychology of Growth, Balance and Harmony* (Wheaton, IL: Quest Books, 1999), pp. 10–11.

25 Guy Murchie, *The Seven Mysteries of Life* (Boston: Houghton Mifflin, A Mariner Book, 1999), pp. 494–519.

26 P.V. Beck, A. L. Walters, and N. Francisco, *The Sacred: Ways of Knowledge, Sources of Life* (Tsaile, AZ: Navajo Community College Press, 1992), pp. 57–63.

27 "Earth Teach Me to Remember," quoted in *The World's Wisdom: Sacred Texts of the World's Religions*, Philip Novak, ed. (New York: HarperCollins, 1995), p. 369.

28 Wayne Muller, *How, Then, Shall We Live?* (New York: Bantam, 1996, p. 194), 197–99.

29 'Abdu'l-Baha, *The Promulgation of Universal Peace: Talks Delivered by 'Abdu'l-Baha during His Visit the United States and Canada in 1912* (Wilmette, IL: Baha'i Publishing Trust, 1982), p. 244. ('Abdu'l-Baha was the son and

authorized interpreter of Baha'u'llah, who was the founder of the Baha'i Faith.) See also, Helen Hornby, compiler, *Lights of Guidance: A Baha'i Reference File* (Wilmette, IL: Baha'i Publishing Trust, 1988), p. 505.

30 Nader Saiedi, *Logos and Civilization: Spirit, History, and Order in the Writings of Baha'u'llah* (Bethesda, MD: University Press of Maryland, 2000), p. 135.

31 Baha'u'llah, *The Hidden Words of Baha'u'llah* (Wilmette, IL: Baha'i Publishing Trust, 1985), p. 33; *Kitab-i-Aqdas* (Haifa: Baha'i World Center, 1992), p. 35; *Gleanings from the Writings of Baha'u'llah* (Wilmette, IL: Baha'i Publishing Trust, 1990), p. 313.

32 For a very clear and insightful analysis of the similarities in the lives of the prophet-founders of the world religions, see Moojan Momem, *The Phenomenon of Religion* (Oxford: Oneworld Publications, 1999), 301–316.

33 R. Frager, *Heart, Self, & Soul*, p. 108.

34 Rumi: "What I Tell About Me," quoted in Andrew Harvey, translator, *Speaking Flame* (Ithaca: Meeramma, 1989).

35 Walt Whitman, "Song of Myself," in *The Complete Poems* (New York: Penguin Classics, 2005), p. 63.

36 Baha'u'llah, *Tablets of Baha'u'llah* (Wilmette, IL: Baha'i Publishing Trust, 1988), pp. 60, 155.

37 Baha'u'llah, *The Hidden Words of Baha'u'llah* (Wilmette, IL: Baha'i Publishing Trust, 1985), p. 37.

38 Reprinted from Doug Lipman, *The Storytelling Coach, How to Listen, Praise, and Bring Out People's Best* (Atlanta, GA: August House, 2006) (see also http://hasidicstories.com/Stories/Other_Early_Rebbes/zusia.html)

CHAPTER 2: Life Is an Eternal Journey

39 'Abdu'l-Baha, *The Promulgation of Universal* Peace (Wilmette, IL: Baha'i Publishing Trust, 1982), p. 335.

40 P.V. Beck, A. L. Walters, and N. Francisco, *The Sacred: Ways of Knowledge, Sources of Life* (Tsaile, AZ: Navajo Community College Press:1992), pp. 189, 198, 205.

41 see the following—For psychosexual development, Sigmund Freud, *An Outline of Psychoanalysis* (New York: Norton, 1949). For cognitive development, Jean Piaget, *Six Psychological Studies* (New York: Random House, 1967). For psychosocial development, Erik Erikson, *Childhood and Society* (New York: Norton, 1963). For moral development, Lawrence

Kohlberg, "Moral Stages and Moralization: The Cognitive-Developmental Approach," in *Moral Development and Behavior: Theory, Research, and Social Issues,* edited by T. Lickona (Austin, TX: Holt, Rinehart & Winston, 1976). For faith development: James Fowler, *Stages of Faith: The Psychology of Human Development and the Quest for Meaning* (San Francisco: Harper, 1981), and Carol Gilligan, *In a Different Voice* (Cambridge: Harvard, 1982). For analytical psychology: C. G. Jung, *Psychology and Education* (Princeton: Princeton University Press, 1969) and C. G. Jung, "Basic Postulates of Analytical Psychology," (1934), in *Collected Works*, Volume 8, *The Structure and Dynamics of the Psyche* (Princeton: Princeton University Press, 1969). For humanistic psychology: Abraham Maslow, *The Farther Reaches of Human Nature* (New York: Penguin, 1976); and Abraham Maslow, *Religion Values and Peak Experiences* (New York: Penguin, 1976). For transpersonal psychology, Ken Wilber, Jack Engler, and Daniel Brown, *The Transformations of Consciousness: Conventional and Contemplative Perspectives on* Development (Boston: Shambhala: 1986); see also, Ken Wilber, *The Atman Project: A Transpersonal View of Human Development* (Wheaton, IL: Theosophical Publishing House, 1980).

42 From Judaism, "The dust returns to the ground it came from, and the spirit returns to God who gave it" (Ecclesiastes 12:7). From Christianity, "Now we know that if the earthly tent we live in is destroyed, we have a building from God, an eternal house in heaven, not built by human hands" (II Corinthians 4:1). From Islam, "Unto Him shall ye return, all together; the promise of God is sure" (Qur'an 10:4). From the Baha'i Faith, "'Verily, we are God's,' and abide within the exalted habitation: 'And unto Him do we return.'" (Baha'u'llah, *Kitab-i-Iqan*. Wilmette, IL: Baha'i Publishing Trust, 1989), p. 90.

43 Quoted in Stephen Mitchell, *The Essence of Wisdom* (New York: Broadway Books, 1998), p. 82.

44 Evelyn Underhill, *Practical Mysticism* (Columbus, OH: Ariel Press, 1986).

45 Evelyn Underhill, *Mysticism: A Study in the Nature and Development of Man's Spiritual* Consciousness (New York. Dutton, 1961), especially Part Two, chapters I–X.

46 Robert Atkinson, *The Gift of Stories: Practical and Spiritual Applications of Autobiography, Life Stories and Personal Mythmaking* (Westport, CT: Bergin & Garvey, 1995), pp. 26, 30–32, 96.

47 Evelyn Underhill, *Mysticism*, p. 437. An important distinction can be made between mystics who view this "union" with Reality as the final goal, and who tend to stress the experience of union itself, even the ecstasy of it, usually more evident among the Sufis, and those who possess a deep conviction and commitment to ongoing active work in the world.

48 The preface to *The Seven Valleys* explains how the Bab (meaning "Gate") and Baha'u'llah (meaning "Glory of God") were independent prophets and the central figures of the Baha'i Faith, which emerged out of Islam in Persia during the 19th century, much as John the Baptist and Christ had emerged out of Judaism nearly 20 centuries earlier. Baha'u'llah's life was one of sacrifice, suffering, enlightenment, withdrawal, union, persecution, and exile. He is the only prophet of God to have left an extensive set of spiritual and social teachings, written and preserved in his own hand, *The Seven Valleys and the Four Valleys* (Wilmette, IL: Baha'i Publishing Trust, 1973). Also http://reference.bahai.org/en/t/bsvfv It is further important to note that *The Seven Valleys* is a response to questions from a Sufi about a difference in understanding of the means of achieving mystic union. Baha'u'llah employed a framework familiar to Sufis from Attar's *Language of the Birds*, while also drawing from the Qur'an, to describe and clarify the ascent of the soul toward the source of its being. Both versions of the journey of the soul through seven valleys explain the stages that include spiritual trials leading to a new consciousness and a transformation of the self. They share the same first three valleys: search, love, and knowledge, describing the soul's quest on the physical plane, and are the same in all the world's religions. Baha'u'llah adds, however, that the Faith of God is changeless and that guidance from a prophet is necessary to progress along the straight path to reunion with God, and further that "the coming of the Divine Manifestation in His Day makes further search unnecessary" (pp. 16–17).

49 Baha'u'llah, The Seven Valleys and the Four Valleys, pp. xi–xii. Thus, the Baha'i perspective views the goal of mystic union as allegorical or metaphorical, rather than literal. The journey through the seven valleys, toward union, is meant to describe the increasing intensity of the process of realizing the spiritual nearness to God, which comes through the knowledge of God, via knowledge of God's prophets, rather than by literal physical union with God.

50 'Abdu'l-Baha, *Some Answered Questions* (Wilmette, IL: Baha'i Pub. Trust, 1990), p. 300.

51 Jalil Mahmoudi, "Irfan, Gnosis, or Mystical Knowledge," in *World Order*, Vol. 7, No. 4, Summer 1973, pp. 5–15.

52 Quoted in Andrew Harvey, *The Direct Path* (New York: Broadway Books, 2000), p. 33. Robert Atkinson and Patricia Locke, "The Lakota View of the Child," *Maine Scholar*, Fall, 1995, pp. 207–220. Hindu scripture, quoted in Andrew Harvey, *The Essential Mystics* (New York: Harper Collins, 1996), p. 40.

53 Robert Frager, *Heart, Self, & Soul: The Sufi Psychology of Growth, Balance, and Harmony* (Wheaton, IL: Quest Books, 1999), pp. 109–111.

54 See D. L. Carmody and J. T. Carmody, *Mysticism: Holiness East and West* (New York: Oxford University Press, 1996), p. 260. The concept of the human life cycle in terms of this curve was first suggested by Tahereh Adieh.

55 Carmody & Carmody, *Mysticism*, p. 260.

56 P.V. Beck, A. L. Walters, and N. Francisco, *The Sacred: Ways of Knowledge, Sources of Life* (Tsaile, AZ: Navajo Community College Press, 1992), p. 198.

PART II Introduction and CHAPTER 3: The Pattern of Transformation

57 Erich Neumann, *Depth Psychology and a New Ethic* (New York: Putnam, 1969), p. 143.

58 C. G. Jung, quoted in Jolande Jacobi, *The Psychology of C. G. Jung* (New Haven: Yale University Press, 1973), pp. 53–54.

59 Thomas Moore, *Dark Nights of the Soul* (New York: Gotham, 2005).

60 A. C. Swinburne, "Atalanta in Calydon," quoted in *The Great Thoughts*, George Seldes, compiler (New York: Ballantine Books, 1985), p. 404.

61 Mircea Eliade, *The Two and the One* (Chicago: University of Chicago Press, 1962), pp. 120–122.

62 C. H. Waddington, *The Strategy of the Genes* (London: Allen & Unwin, 1957).

63 Arnold van Gennep, *The Rites of Passage* (Chicago: University of Chicago Press, 1960).

64 Joseph Campbell, *Myths to Live By* (New York: Viking, 1972), p. 211.

65 Erik Erikson, *Childhood and Society* (New York: Norton, 1950).

66 Deepak Chopra, *The Book of Secrets* (New York: Harmony Books, 2004), pp. 1–3, 108–110.

67 Baha'u'llah, *Gleanings From the Writings of Baha'u'llah.* (Wilmette, IL: Baha'i Publishing Trust, 1990), pp. 100, 72.

68 Jolande Jacobi, *The Psychology of C. G. Jung*, pp. 53, 55; C. G. Jung, *Memories, Dreams, Reflections*, pp. 345, 311, 335.

69 C. G. *Jung, Memories, Dreams, Reflections* (New York: Random House, 1963), pp. 392–93. See also Jolande Jacobi, *The Psychology of C. G. Jung* (New Haven: Yale University Press), 1973, pp. 47–49 and Jolande Jacobi, *Complex Archetype Symbol in the Psychology of C. G. Jung* (Princeton: Princeton University Press, 1974), pp. 31–73; and June Singer, *Boundaries of the Soul* (New York: Anchor Books), 1994, pp. 44, 100.

70 C. G. Jung, "Archetypes of the Collective Unconscious," in *The Archetypes and the Collective Unconscious* (Princeton: Princeton University Press, 1959), Collected Works, Vol. 9, Part 1, pp. 5, 28.

71 C. G. Jung, *Psychological Reflections* (Princeton: Princeton University Press, 1970), pp. 38–39.

72 Jacobi, Complex Archetype Symbol, p. 65; also Anthony Storr, ed., The Essential Jung (Princeton: Princeton University Press, 1983), pp. 16, 25.

73 For a more detailed discussion of myth, ritual, and archetype, and how their forms are all metaphors of transformation, see Robert Atkinson, *The Gift of Stories: Practical and Spiritual Applications of Autobiography, Life Stories, and Personal Mythmaking* (Westport, CT.: Bergin & Garvey, 1995), especially, pp. 25–47. See also, Jacobi, T*he Psychology of C. G. Jung*, p. 67.

74 For a clear and concise discussion of the spiritual journey as moral development and self-actualization, see Nader Saiedi, *Logos and Civilization: Spirit, History, and Order in the Writings of Baha'u'llah* (Bethesda, MD: University Press of Maryland, 2000); 100–102.

75 'Abdu'l-Baha, *Paris Talks* (London: Baha'i Publishing Trust, 1971), p. 178.

76 Baha'u'llah, *Gleanings from the Writings of Baha'u'llah* (Wilmette, IL: Baha'i Publishing Trust, 1990), p. 129.

77 'Abdu'l-Baha, *Selections from the Writings of 'Abdu'l-Baha.* (Haifa: Baha'i World Centre, 1988), p. 157.

78 Plato, *The Republic* (New York: Oxford University Press, 1958), pp. 229–231.

79 John Hatcher, *The Purpose of Physical Reality* (Wilmette, IL: Baha'i Publishing Trust, 1987), pp. 7–14; 27–29.

80 Baha'u'llah, *The Hidden Words of Baha'u'llah* (Wilmette, IL: Baha'i Publishing Trust, 1975), pp. 6–7; Gleanings, 65–66.

81 Joseph Henderson, "Ancient Myths and Modern Man," in C. G Jung, Man and His Symbols (New York: Laurel/Dell, 1968), pp. 110–111. Everyone

carries a shadow: Jolande Jacobi, *The Psychology of C. G. Jung* (New Haven: Yale University Press, 1973), 109–114; also, Jung, *Man and His Symbols*, pp. 171–185. All that is within us that we do not know about: Marie-Louise von Franz, *Shadow and Evil in Fairy Tales* (Boston: Shambhala, 1995), pp. 3–6. Acceptance of the shadow: Erich Neumann, *Depth Psychology and a New Ethic* (New York: Putnam, 1969), pp. 143, 146–147.

82 Guy Murchie, *The Seven Mysteries of Life.* (Boston: Houghton Mifflin, 1999), pp. 486–87.

83 'Abdu'l-Baha, *Some Answered Questions*, p. 257; see also Dan Millman, *The Laws of Spirit* (Tiburon, CA: H. J. Kramer, 1995), pp. 9–16.

CHAPTER 4: The Soul Is in the Depths

84 Joseph Campbell, *The Hero with a Thousand Faces* (Princeton: Princeton University Press, 1949), p. 25.

85 Chief Leon Shenandoah, quoted in *The Essential Mystics: Selections From the World's Great Wisdom Traditions*, A. Harvey, ed. (San Francisco: HarperCollins, 1996), p. 6.

86 C. G. Jung, *Memories, Dreams, Reflections* (New York: Vintage, 1963), pp. vi–xii, 3–5.

87 Robert Atkinson, *Remembering 1969: Searching for the Eternal in Changing Times* (Wilmette, IL: Baha'i Publishing Trust, 2008).

88 lecture by Joseph Campbell: Published as Chapter 10 in Joseph Campbell, *Myths to Live By* (New York: Viking, 1972).

89 Joseph Campbell, *The Hero with a Thousand* Faces, p. 30.

90 C. G. Jung, Memories, Dreams, Reflections (New York: Vintage Books, 1961), p. 392.

91 Jean Bolen spoke of "moments of truth" in a talk given in Portland, Maine, April 12, 1991, "The Hero and Heroine in Everyperson: The Mythic Dimensions of Ordinary Life," sponsored by the C. G. Jung Center, Brunswick, Maine.

92 J. Campbell, *The Hero with a Thousand Faces,* especially pp. 49–243; R. Atkinson, *The Gift of Stories: Practical and Spiritual Applications of Autobiography, Life Stories, and Personal Mythmaking* (Westport, CT.: Bergin & Garvey, 1995), especially ch. 5, pp. 83–106, where I have adapted Campbell's monomyth to contemporary settings for the purpose of personal mythmaking.

93 For a discussion of reconceptualizing the idea of return in relation to *The Seven Valleys,* see N. Saiedi, *Logos and Civilization: Spirit, History, and Order in*

the Writings of Baha'u'llah (Bethesda: University Press of Maryland, 2000), pp. 66–69.

94 Ruhiyyih Rabbani, The Priceless Pearl (London: Baha'i Publishing Trust, 1969), pp. 118–124.

95 Attributed to 'Abdu'l-Baha, in Myron H. Phelps, *The Life and Teachings of Abbas Effendi* (New York: G. P. Putnam/Knickerbocker Press, 1903), pp. 159–164.

96 Robert Frager, *Heart, Self, & Soul: The Sufi Psychology of Growth, Balance and Harmony* (Wheaton, IL: Quest Books, 1999), pp. 2–63.

97 'Abdu'l-Baha, *Selected Writings of 'Abdu'l-Baha* (Haifa: Baha'i World Center, 1978), p. 96.

98 Baha'u'llah, *Gleanings from the Writings of Baha'u'llah* (Wilmette, IL: Baha'i Publishing Trust, 1983), p. 149.

99 Joseph Campbell, The Hero with a Thousand Faces, p. 30.

Part III Introduction and CHAPTER 5: At Our Depths We Are All Connected

100 Rumi, "The Lamps Are Different," *The Rumi Collection*, Kabir Helminski, ed. (Boston: Shambhala, 1998), pp. 137–138.

101 Baha'u'llah, *Tablets of Baha'u'llah* (Wilmette, IL: Baha'i Publishing Trust, 1998), p. 219.

102 'Abdu'l-Baha, *The Promulgation of Universal Peace* (Wilmette, IL: Baha'i Publishing Trust, 1982), p. 172; *Some Answered Questions* (Wilmette, IL: Baha'i Publishing Trust, 1981), p. 199.

103 'Abdu'l-Baha, 'Abdu'l-Baha in London (Wilmette, IL: Baha'i Publishing Trust, 1984), p. 27.

104 Abdu'l-Baha, *The Promulgation of Universal Peace,* pp. 97–98; Foundations of World Unity (Wilmette, IL: Baha'i Publishing Trust, 1972), p. 81.

105 Baha'u'llah, *Gleanings from the Writings of Baha'u'llah* (Wilmette, IL: Baha'i Publishing Trust, 1983), p. 136. See also *The Compilation of Compilations,* compiled by the Research Department of the Universal House of Justice (Mona Vale: Baha'i Publishing Australia, 1991), vol. I, p. 22.

106 For a more detailed discussion on our purpose and the direction of our evolution, see chapters 2 and 9, especially, in Ruhiyyih Rabbani, *Prescription for Living* (George Ronald, Publisher, Oxford, 1989).

107 See "The Hidden Words" and "Gleanings" of Baha'u'llah, in *The Reality of Man* (Wilmette, IL: Baha'i Publishing, 2005), pp. 9–16.

108 Huston Smith, *The Illustrated World's Religions* (New York: Harper San Francisco, 1994), pp. 10–14.

109 ibid.

110 Quoted in Jeffery Moses (ed.) *Oneness: Great Principles Shared by All Religions* (New York: Ballantine Books, 2002), pp. 127–129.

111 ibid.

112 'Abdu'l-Baha, quoted in *The Reality of Man* (Wilmette, IL: Baha'i Publishing, 2005), pp. 35–36.

113 Moojan Momen, *The Phenomenon of Religion: A Thematic Approach* (Oxford: Oneworld Publications, 1999), pp. 268–275.

114 Rumi, quoted in James Fadiman and Robert Frager, eds. Essential Sufism (New York: HarperOne, 1999), p. 75.

115 Hans Kung and Karl-Josef Kuschel, eds. *A Global Ethic: The Declaration of the Parliament of the World's Religions* (New York: Continuum, 1998), pp. 17; 13–16.

116 ibid.

117 'Abdu'l-Baha, *The Promulgation of Universal Peace*, p. 157.

118 Hans Kung, *A Global Ethic*, pp. 34–36.

119 Robert Wright, *Nonzero: The Logic of Human Destiny.* (New York: Vintage Books, 2001), especially pp. 308–324.

120 Quoted in Jeffery Moses (ed.) *Oneness: Great Principles Shared by All Religions*, pp. 15–17.

121 'Abdu'l-Baha, *The Promulgation of Universal Peace*, 173.

122 'Abdu'l-Baha, *'Abdu'l-Baha in London* (Wilmette, IL: Baha'i Publishing Trust, 1984), p. 29.

123 Quoted in Andrew Harvey (ed.) *The Essential Mystics: Selections from the World's Great Wisdom Traditions* (New York: HarperSanFrancisco, 1997), pp. 102–103.

124 Rumi, "I Know Nothing of Two Worlds," *A Garden Beyond Paradise*, Jonathan Star and Shahram Shiva, trans. (New York: Bantam Books, 1992).

125 Jolande Jacobi, *The Psychology of C. G. Jung* (New Haven: Yale University Press, 1973), pp. 67, 137.

126 Quoted in Andrew Harvey (ed.) *The Essential Mystics: Selections from the World's Great Wisdom Traditions* (New York: HarperSanFrancisco, 1997), pp. 50–52.

127 Baha'u'llah, *The Seven Valleys and the Four Valleys* (Wilmette, IL: Baha'i Publishing Trust, 1975), pp. 17, 24–25.

128 ibid, 15.

129 *The Prosperity of Humankind*, published by the Baha'i International Community (Wilmette, IL: Baha'i Publishing Trust, 1995), pp. 3–4.

130 'Abdu'l-Baha, *Selections from the Writings of 'Abdu'l-Baha* (Haifa: Baha'i World Center, 1978), pp. 260–261; and *The Promulgation of Universal Peace*, pp. 129–130.

131 'Abdu'l-Baha, *Selections from the Writings of 'Abdu'l-Baha,* p. 76.

132 Nader Saiedi, *Logos and Civilization: Spirit, History, and Order in the Writings of Baha'u'llah* (Bethesda, MD: University Press of Maryland, 2000), pp. 106–107.

133 Jeffery Moses (ed.) Oneness: Great Principles Shared by All Religions, pp. xi–xvii.

134 U.N. Declaration on the Rights of Indigenous Peoples: http://www.un.org/esa/socdev/unpfii/en/drip.html

135 *The Reality of Man: Excerpts from the Writings of Baha'u'llah and 'Abdu'l-Baha* (Wilmette, IL: Baha'i Publishing, 2005), pp. 3–4.

136 William C. Chittick (trans.) *The Sufi Path of Love: The Spiritual Teachings of Rumi* (Albany: State University of New York Press, 1983), 122.

137 Baha'u'llah, Gleanings from the Writings of Baha'u'llah, p. 215.

CHAPTER 6: Soul-Making Is Part of Our Sacred Heritage

138 Rumi, "We Are All the Same," in *Love Poems of Rumi* (Kansas City, MO: Andrews McMeel, 2002), p. 16.

139 Fakhruddin Iraqi, "Love," quoted in Philip Novak, in *The World's Wisdom: Sacred Texts of the World's Religions* (New York: Harper Collins, 1995), pp. 329–330.

140 Robert Butler, "Age, Death and Life Review," See: http://www.hospicefoundation.org/pages/page.asp?page_id=171322

141 Robert Butler, *Why Survive? Being Old in America* (New York: Harper, 1975), p. 415.

142 Robert Weller, *The Bridges of Madison County* (New York: Warner Books, 1992).

143 "Love," Fakhruddin Iraqi, quoted in Novak, *The World's Wisdom*, pp. 329–330.

144 Quoted in *Oneness: Great Principles Shared by all Religions*, Jeffrey Moses, ed. (New York: Ballantine Books, 2002), pp. 33–35.

145 Patricia Locke, from a talk given at the University of Southern Maine, Portland, Maine, 1992, videotaped by and archived in the Life Story Center, USM. 1992-05-001.

146 Thich Nhat Hanh, Peace *Is Every Step* (New York: Bantam Books, 1991), p. 74.

147 Wayne Muller: *How, Then, Shall We Live* (New York: Bantam, 1996), pp. 69–85.

148 Quoted in *Oneness: Great Principles Shared by all Religions*, edited by Jeffrey Moses (New York: Ballantine Books, 2002), pp. 88–90.

149 See Universal House of Justice, *Messages from the Universal House of Justice: 1963–1986* (Wilmette, IL: Baha'i Publishing Trust, 1996), p. 589. Shoghi Effendi, quoted in *Spiritual Foundations: Prayer, Meditation, and the Devotional Attitude.* (Wilmette, IL: Baha'i Publishing Trust, 1980), p. 17. Shoghi Effendi quoted in *Importance of Deepening Our Knowledge and Understanding of the Faith.* (Ontario, Canada: Baha'i Community of Canada, 1983), p. 232.

150 Joseph Campbell, *The Hero with a Thousand* Faces (Princeton, NJ: Princeton University Press, 1949), p. 25.

151 C. G. Jung, *The Spirit in Man, Art, and Literature.* (Princeton, NJ: Princeton University Press, 1971), p. 82.

152 C. G. Jung, *Memories, Dreams, Reflections* (New York: Vintage Books, 1963), p. 171.

153 Martin Luther King Jr., *A Call to Conscience: The Landmark Speeches of Dr. Martin Luther King Jr.*, Clay Carson and Kris Shepard, eds. (New York: Warner Books, 2001), pp. 160–61.

154 John Neihardt, *Black Elk Speaks* (New York: Simon & Schuster, 1959), p. 6.

155 Margaret Mead, *Culture and Commitment* (New York: Anchor Press/ Doubleday, 1978).

156 Erik Erikson, *A Way of Looking at Things: The Collected Papers of Erik Erikson,* Stephen P. Schlein, ed. (New York: Norton, 1987).

157 Joseph Campbell, *The Masks of God*, Vol. 4, *Creative Mythology* (New York: Viking, 1970), p. xx.

158 Rollo May, *Rollo May on Existential Psychology* (Film, American Personnel and Guidance Association, Alexandria, VA., 1976).

159 Ervin Laszlo, *You Can Change the World* (Shropshire, U.K.: Positive News Publishing, 2002), p. 80.

160 James Redfield and Michael Murphy, *God and the Evolving Universe: The Next Step in Personal Evolution* (New York: Tarcher, 2002), pp. 129–136.

161 Baha'i World Center, Commissioned by the Universal House of Justice, *One Common Faith* (Haifa: Baha'i World Center, 2005).

162 Peter Russell, *The Global Brain: Speculations on the Evolutionary Leap to Planetary Consciousness* (Los Angeles: Tarcher, 1983).

163 Robert Wright, *Nonzero: The Logic of Human Destiny* (New York: Vintage Books, 2001) pp. 51, 191–92, 301–332.

164 Robert Johnson, *Femininity Lost and Regained* (New York: Harper & Row, 1990), pp. 95–97.

INDEX

ABOUT THE AUTHOR

Robert Atkinson, Ph.D., is an internationally recognized authority in helping people tell their life stories. He is a pioneer in the development of the life story interview methodology and among the first to apply Joseph Campbell's classic work on the mythological journey of the hero to contemporary personal mythmaking. His two books in these areas have been translated into three languages and are widely used in various personal growth and life review settings.

He is a professor of human development and religious studies, director of the Life Story Center, senior research fellow in the OLLI National Resource Center at the University of Southern Maine, and the author, co-author, or editor of eight books, including his memoir, *Remembering 1969: Searching for the Eternal in Changing Times* (2008); an autobiography with Babatunde Olatunji, *The Beat of My Drum* (2005); *The Life Story Interview* (1998); and *The Gift of Stories* (1995). He has a Ph.D. in cross-cultural human development from the University of Pennsylvania, an M.A. in American Folk Culture from the Cooperstown Graduate Program, SUNY, an M.A. in Counseling from the University of New Hampshire, and a B.A. in Philosophy and American Studies from Long Island University, Southampton.

In previous books, Atkinson explored personal storytelling from a psychological and cultural perspective. With *Mystic Journey*, he explores soul-making from a multi-faith, eternal perspective. He can be found online at *www.RobertAtkinson.net.*

CPSIA information can be obtained at www.ICGtesting.com
Printed in the USA
BVOW042042120712

295069BV00001B/4/P

9 781616 407155